STUART MCHARDY is a w............................d
sometime tippler. Havin.................................of
Scottish culture through.................................e,
history, folklore – he has...............................er
of a century. McHardy....................................s,
jazz and rock in many o...................................g
with his life on several..................................d
heritage of his native land has been honed by many hours of discussion
with a range of interesting individuals in many of the locales covered
in this book. Over the years much of Scotland's artistic and cultural life
has revolved around pubs and this will doubtless continue. Although
he has held some illustrious positions including Director of the Scots
Language Resource Centre and President of the Pictish Arts Society,
McHardy is probably proudest of having been a member of the Vigil
for a Scottish Parliament. To date he has published *Strange Secrets of
Ancient Scotland, Tales of Whisky and Smuggling, The Wild Haggis and the
Greetin Faced Nyaff* and *Scotland: Myth, Legend and Folklore*, the latter for
the same slave-driving despot who publishes this small volume.
McHardy lives very near the centre of Edinburgh with the beautiful
Sandra and their talented son Roderick.

To the memory of Sydney Goodsir Smith, poet and celebrant of Bacchanalia. His magnificent work Carotid Cornucopius was a constant inspiration in the compiling of this humbler tome.

Edinburgh and Leith Pub Guide

STUART McHARDY

Luath Press Limited

EDINBURGH

www.luath.co.uk

First Published 2000

The paper used in this book is recyclable. It is made from low
chlorine pulps produced in a low energy, low emission manner
from renewable forests.

Printed and bound by
Omnia Books Ltd., Glasgow

Typeset in 10 point Dante and 8 point Franklin Gothic by
S. Fairgrieve, Edinburgh

Design by Tom Bee

Maps by Jim Lewis

Illustrations by Nic Geard

Contents

PUBS THAT ARE INCLUDED in this wee book have been carefully chosen by the author, whose long career as a denizen of the Capital's drinking dens has given him a particular, some might suggest twisted, view of what makes a good pub. Basically this is that the hostelry concerned does what it sets out to do – i.e. provide its customers with what they want. So if a pub aims itself at a young or student clientele and does so with style and efficiency, it is considered just as good as traditional ale house that perhaps hearkens back to an older tradition of relaxed and quiet drinking. Sadly one or two bars that satisfy their clientele rather well but have allowed standards to slip – by, perhaps, developing an idiosyncratic relationship with cleanliness – have been left out as the author feels he cannot recommend them to visitors to our city.

There has been a deliberate attempt to include as wide a range of pubs as possible in this book and whatever your tastes you should find something to suit you here. The new trend towards bistros and café-bar venues has largely been ignored in these pages. This a pub guide! A word of warning: the pubs are arranged by area but the publishers cannot accept responsibility for any misguided attempts to drink in every one of the pubs in any one area in any one session.

Comments received by the author on the inclusion or otherwise, or rating, of individual pubs may be reflected in future editions. Attempts by publicans to sway his judgement with copious quantities of his favourite tipple are unlikely to succeed.

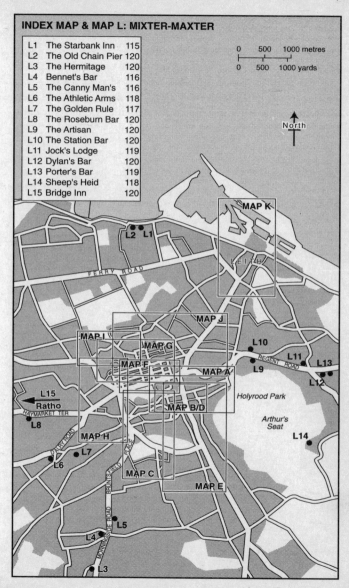

8

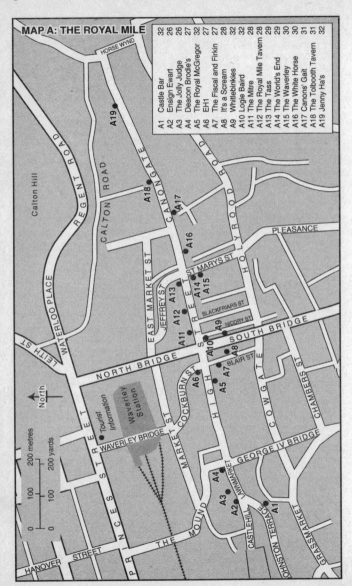

MAP A: THE ROYAL MILE

A1	Castle Bar	32
A2	Ensign Ewart	26
A3	The Jolly Judge	26
A4	Deacon Brodie's	27
A5	The Royal McGregor	32
A6	EH1	27
A7	The Fiscal and Firkin	27
A8	It's a Scream	28
A9	Whitebinkies	32
A10	Logie Baird	32
A11	The Mitre	28
A12	The Royal Mile Tavern	28
A13	The Tass	29
A14	The World's End	29
A15	The Waverley	30
A16	The White Horse	30
A17	Canons' Gait	31
A18	The Tolbooth Tavern	31
A19	Jenny Ha's	32

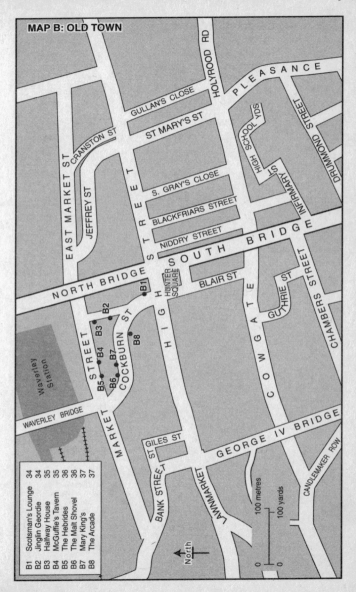

MAP B: OLD TOWN

HOLYROOD RD

PLEASANCE

GULLAN'S CLOSE

ST MARY'S ST

CRANSTON ST

HIGH SCHOOL YDS

DRUMMOND STREET

EAST MARKET ST

S. GRAY'S CLOSE

INFIRMARY ST

JEFFREY ST

BLACKFRIARS STREET

NIDDRY STREET

ST MARY'S STREET

SOUTH BRIDGE

NORTH BRIDGE

BLAIR ST

HUNTER SQUARE

B1

B2

B3

COCKBURN ST

B4

B8

GUTHRIE ST

CHAMBERS STREET

B7

B5 B6

HIGH STREET

COWGATE

Waverley Station

MARKET STREET

WAVERLEY BRIDGE

GILES ST

GEORGE IV BRIDGE

BANK STREET

LAWNMARKET

CANDLEMAKER ROW

100 metres

100 yards

B1 Scotsman's Lounge   34
B2 Jinglin Geordie   34
B3 Halfway House   35
B4 McGuffie's Tavern   35
B5 The Hebrides   36
B6 The Malt Shovel   36
B7 Mary King's   37
B8 The Arcade   37

0

0

North

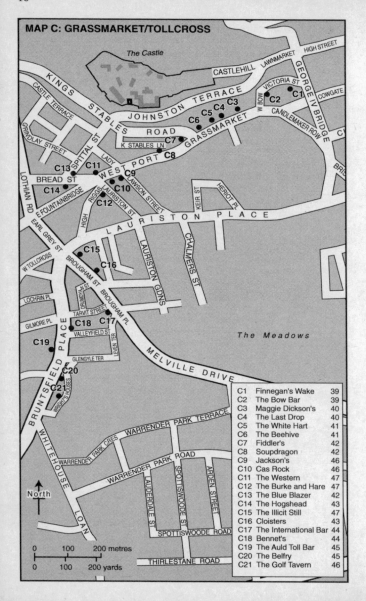

MAP C: GRASSMARKET/TOLLCROSS

The Castle

C1	Finnegan's Wake	39
C2	The Bow Bar	39
C3	Maggie Dickson's	40
C4	The Last Drop	40
C5	The White Hart	41
C6	The Beehive	41
C7	Fiddler's	42
C8	Soupdragon	42
C9	Jackson's	46
C10	Cas Rock	46
C11	The Western	47
C12	The Burke and Hare	47
C13	The Blue Blazer	42
C14	The Hogshead	43
C15	The Illicit Still	47
C16	Cloisters	43
C17	The International Bar	44
C18	Bennet's	44
C19	The Auld Toll Bar	45
C20	The Belfry	45
C21	The Golf Tavern	46

North

0   100   200 metres
0   100   200 yards

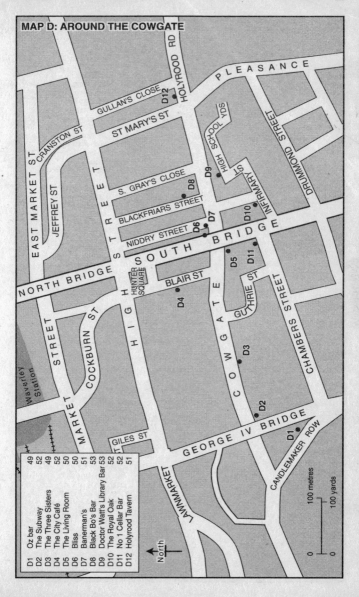

MAP D: AROUND THE COWGATE

PLEASANCE

HOLYROOD RD

GULLAN'S CLOSE

D12

ST MARY'S ST

HIGH SCHOOL YDS

CRANSTON ST

EAST MARKET ST

JEFFREY ST

DRUMMOND STREET

S. GRAY'S CLOSE

D8

D9

BLACKFRIARS STREET

INFIRMARY ST

INFIRMARY STREET

D7

D6

NIDDRY STREET

D10

HIGH STREET

SOUTH BRIDGE

NORTH BRIDGE

HUNTER SQUARE

D5 D11

BLAIR ST

D4

COWGATE

GUTHRIE ST

CHAMBERS STREET

D3

COCKBURN ST

MARKET STREET

Waverley Station

GILES ST

D2

GEORGE IV BRIDGE

D1

CANDLEMAKER ROW

LAWNMARKET

North

D1	Oz bar	49
D2	The Subway	52
D3	The Three Sisters	49
D4	The City Café	52
D5	The Living Room	50
D6	Bliss	50
D7	Banerman's	51
D8	Black Bo's Bar	52
D9	Doctor Watt's Library Bar	53
D10	The Royal Oak	52
D11	No 1 Cellar Bar	51
D12	Holyrood Tavern	

0   100 metres
0   100 yards

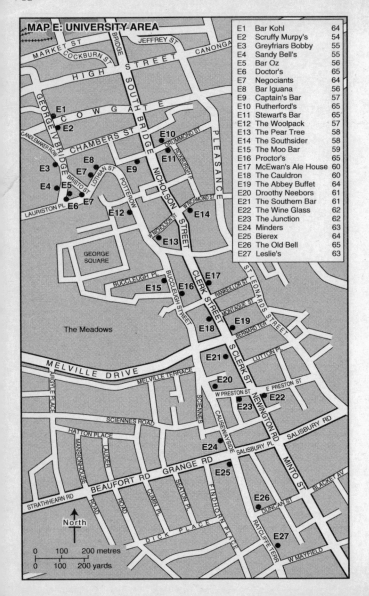

MAP E: UNIVERSITY AREA

E1	Bar Kohl	64
E2	Scruffy Murpy's	54
E3	Greyfriars Bobby	55
E4	Sandy Bell's	55
E5	Bar Oz	56
E6	Doctor's	65
E7	Negociants	64
E8	Bar Iguana	56
E9	Captain's Bar	57
E10	Rutherford's	65
E11	Stewart's Bar	65
E12	The Woolpack	57
E13	The Pear Tree	58
E14	The Southsider	58
E15	The Moo Bar	59
E16	Proctor's	65
E17	McEwan's Ale House	60
E18	The Cauldron	60
E19	The Abbey Buffet	64
E20	Droothy Neebors	61
E21	The Southern Bar	61
E22	The Wine Glass	62
E23	The Junction	62
E24	Minders	63
E25	Bierex	64
E26	The Old Bell	65
E27	Leslie's	63

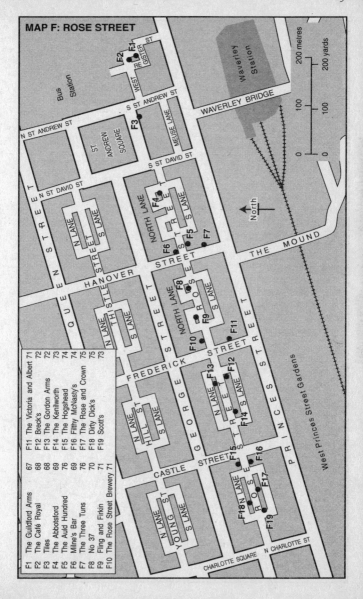

MAP F: ROSE STREET

F1	The Guildford Arms	67
F2	The Café Royal	68
F3	Tiles	68
F4	The Abbotsford	69
F5	The Auld Hundred	76
F6	Milne's Bar	69
F7	The Three Tuns	76
F8	No 37	70
F9	Fling and Firkin	71
F10	The Rose Street Brewery	71
F11	The Victoria and Albert	71
F12	Breck's	72
F13	The Gordon Arms	72
F14	The Kenilworth	73
F15	The Hogshead	74
F16	Filthy McNasty's	74
F17	The Rose and Crown	75
F18	Dirty Dick's	75
F19	Scott's	73

Waverley Station

Bus Station

ST ANDREW SQUARE

WAVERLEY BRIDGE

THE MOUND

West Princes Street Gardens

North

200 metres
200 yards
0   100   200

14

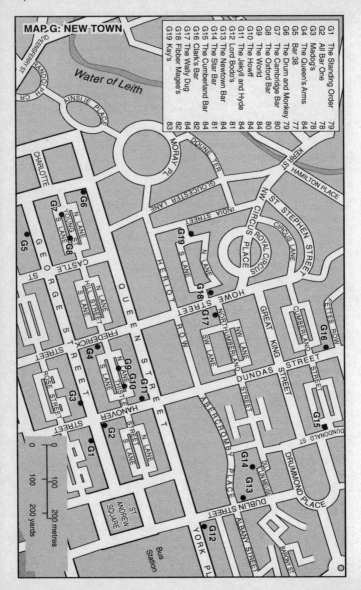

G1 The Standing Order 79
G2 All Bar One 78
G3 Madog's 78
G4 The Queen's Arms 84
G5 Bar 38 77
G6 The Drum and Monkey 79
G7 The Cambridge Bar 84
G8 The Oxford Bar 80
G9 The World 80
G10 The Howff 84
G11 The Jekyll and Hyde 84
G12 Lord Bodo's 81
G13 The Newtown Bar 84
G14 The Star Bar 81
G15 The Cumberland Bar 84
G16 Clark's Bar 82
G17 The Wally Dug 84
G18 Flibber Magee's 82
G19 Kay's 83

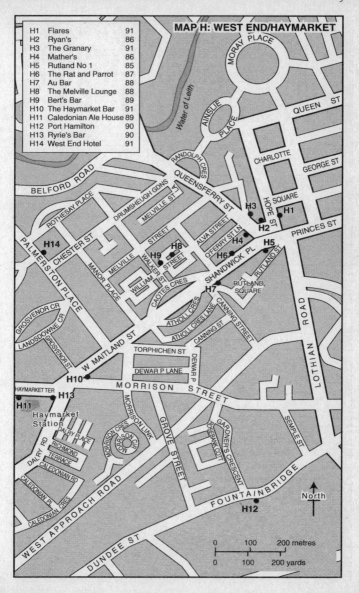

MAP H: WEST END/HAYMARKET

H1	Flares	91
H2	Ryan's	86
H3	The Granary	91
H4	Mather's	86
H5	Rutland No 1	85
H6	The Rat and Parrot	87
H7	Au Bar	88
H8	The Melville Lounge	88
H9	Bert's Bar	89
H10	The Haymarket Bar	91
H11	Caledonian Ale House	89
H12	Port Hamilton	90
H13	Ryrie's Bar	90
H14	West End Hotel	91

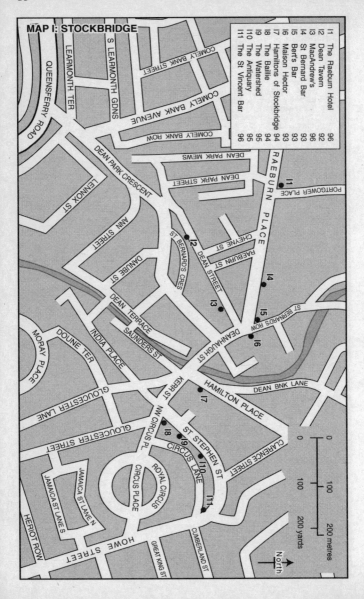

MAP I: STOCKBRIDGE

I1	The Raeburn Hotel	96
I2	Dean Tavern	92
I3	MacAndrew's	96
I4	St Bernard Bar	93
I5	Bert's Bar	93
I6	Maison Hector	93
I7	Hamiltons of Stockbridge	94
I8	The Baillie	94
I9	The Watershed	95
I10	The Antiquary	95
I11	The St Vincent Bar	96

North

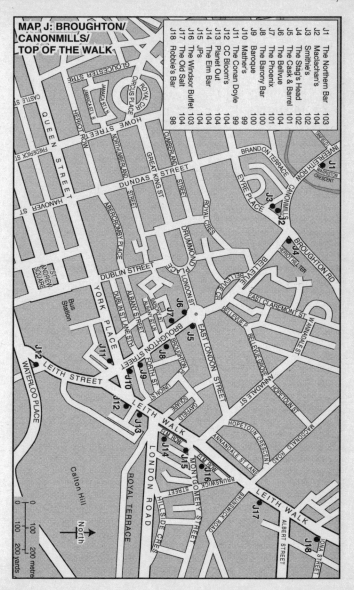

MAP J: BROUGHTON/ CANONMILLS/ TOP OF THE WALK

J1	The Northern Bar	103
J2	Maclachan's	104
J3	Smithie's	102
J4	The Stag's Head	102
J5	The Cask & Barrel	101
J6	The Bellvue	104
J7	The Phoenix	104
J8	The Barony Bar	101
J9	Baroque	100
J10	Mather's	100
J11	The Conan Doyle	99
J12	CC Bloom's	99
J13	Planet Out	104
J14	The Elm Bar	104
J15	JPs	104
J16	The Windsor Buffet	103
J17	The Old Salt	104
J18	Robbie's Bar	98

18

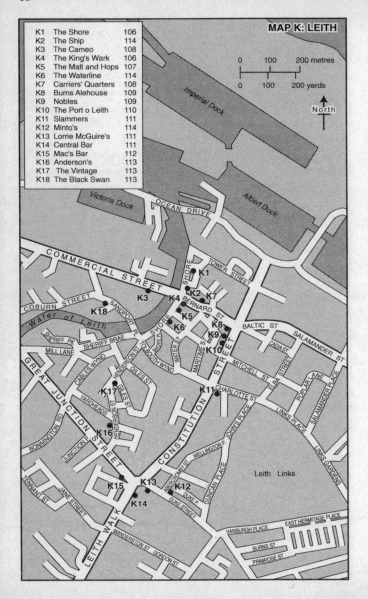

K1	The Shore	106
K2	The Ship	114
K3	The Cameo	108
K4	The King's Wark	106
K5	The Malt and Hops	107
K6	The Waterline	114
K7	Carriers' Quarters	108
K8	Burns Alehouse	109
K9	Nobles	109
K10	The Port o Leith	110
K11	Slammers	111
K12	Minto's	114
K13	Lorrie McGuire's	111
K14	Central Bar	111
K15	Mac's Bar	112
K16	Anderson's	113
K17	The Vintage	113
K18	The Black Swan	113

MAP K: LEITH

Introduction

SCOTLAND AS A NATION has a long history of celebrating with alcoholic drink. Like many other northern countries, we need to have fortification against the rigours of what are all too often vicious winters. While we might not get as much snow as some of our European cousins, like the Finns or the Lapps, we get a different kind of snow. Theirs falls down, ours tends to arrive horizontally, driven by gale force winds straight into the face! This, combined with a particular kind of wet and cold weather, best described in the Scots word dreich (wet, miserable and cold) has led to a centuries-old love affair with whisky, our national drink. However, we also have a long tradition of beer drinking and our predilection for claret and other fine wines derives from a long series of treaties with our French friends that is generally called the Auld Alliance. The sophistication of the Scottish palate should surprise no one. It is one of the interesting aspects of our national character that we can have a high appreciation of fine wines yet still like to get blootered on strong spirits – generally at different times, but not religiously so. The reputation of the Scots for being dour is of course a fabrication by our neighbours to the south. Our conviviality is legendary throughout the world. As most Scots know when travelling abroad, other nationalities always seem to know of our willingness to enter into celebration with or without justification. This international appreciation of our conviviality, particularly when enhanced by the local national drink, has been greatly boosted in recent years by the Tartan Army – the travelling support of our national football team. That is Association Football, known strangely in some odd parts of the world as soccer. The propensity of the Tartan Army to create a tanked up party wherever they go is unlike that of some other supporters, who sadly descend into rage and violence once strong drink is taken.

Scotland is home to the finest of all spirits, whisky. Single malts are truly magnificent, but many people are quite happy to drink the decidedly inferior blended whiskies, which though considerably cheaper will have the same effect. We also brew beers of many kinds, some of which are of mind-blowing strength. We actually have more stouts than the Irish, though they are mainly brewed by small breweries and thus are only available in a few places. There are also a couple of wineries in Scotland and these are innovative in that they will have nothing at all to do with the effete grape. They make a range of wine from a variety of sources including brambles (blackberries), blaeberries – a delectable mountain fruit distantly related to the blueberry, birch sap, elderflowers and other plants that can survive our boisterous climate. Many of these are actually worth drinking, blaeberry wine in some years being as fine as any premier cru claret and a splendid accompaniment to Scottish venison, yum-yum.

While all of Scotland has its drinking traditions, the Capital is of course a bit special. Edinburgh has some of the finest pubs on the planet and though it would never do to encourage the obnoxious habit of pub-crawling, you may find that you have to do a spot of hostelry-hopping to savour more than a soupçon of the delights on offer in Edinburgh and Leith. Leith, though officially part of Edinburgh (since 1920), still retains a sense of its own identity and has a long tradition of maritime brain-bashing with rum and other beverages. Nowadays the Old Port is awash with wine bars and other new-fangled notions, but still has some very fine pubs.

One of the things about Edinburgh is that as Scotland's capital it has for a long time had a considerable professional class – it is loaded with lawyers, crawling with civil servants and mobbed by medics. An old joke has it that you can't get into an Edinburgh pub when the General Assembly of the Church of Scotland is in session, as they are all full of ministers! There is a grain of truth in this as drinking is a sport that in Scotland crosses all political, professional and class lines. Our literature over the past few hundred years is full of drinking songs, tales of prodigious drinking and a general appreciation of the bonhomie of the bottle. Drink has long fuelled the inspiration of our artists and poets, musicians and actors. Long may the tradition continue.

This look at Edinburgh and Leith's hostelries will chance upon some of Scotland's great creative souls, many of whom, though not born in the city, had a grand old time when they came to call. The opinions are the author's, a gentle soul who has been supping the occasional half-pint of beer over the past three decades in many of the pubs herein. Over this period fashions in pubs and drinking have changed – mostly for the better but as you will see not all developments are considered a boon. The extension of opening hours has been a great benefit and begins to bring Scotland into line with European practice, though in this respect Edinburgh is by far and away the most civilised of Scottish cities in terms of late and early opening. The idiotic fantasy of Irish theme pubs seems at last to be fading away. Never have I set foot in a pub in Scotland that was remotely like an Irish one – for a start we still bar our children from our hostelries, as if the very activity of taking a drink was inherently sinful. This is absolute tosh and the upshot is that young people, instead of learning how to control their drink by observing the generally responsible and moderate behaviour of their parents when it comes to drink, wait for the day when they can at last enter the hallowed halls of hospitality – usually considerably before the official drinking age of 18! This is a fact of life that has been constant for generations, but politicians, people who are in the main strangers to common sense and an affront to common decency, still witter on about the problems of under age drinking.

Things have improved on the drinking front generally though, and in these pages you will find a selection of pubs, chosen by the author for one reason or another, that will hopefully provide a selection of the best the Capital has to offer. Whether you like music of a particular type, are a fan of real beer – traditionally fermented twice, enjoy meeting local characters, savour the exciting possibilities of the vast range of single malts available or want to meet people with tastes like your own, there should be something here for you. Anyone reading this book who cannot find a hostelry that they like can write to me, care of the publisher, and I will burn the letter! There is enough information to allow you to dip lightly in waters of hospitality or get roaring fou on any dozens of alcoholic beverages within the boundaries of one of the world's most beautiful and accessible cities. We are fortunate indeed that so much of our fair city survived the brutalism of the various so-called architectural fashions that have blighted so many other cities on this island. Many of our selection of drinking dens can be visited on foot in a short time.

Scotland's greatest poet, Robert Burns, known throughout the world, lived in Edinburgh for a while and enjoyed a drink or two in the local taverns. As we go into the new millennium with a new political system in place, we can do worse than remember one of the toasts he left us with, 'Whisky and Freedom gang thegither, Tak aff yer dram'. This means sup up, so get to it!!!

What like is this pub?

The overall rating for the pubs given here is from 1-5 dugs – a dug being a Scots dog and of course the logo of the publishing house Luath, which is a Gaelic dog's name meaning swift or fast. The number of dugs given depends on general atmosphere and friendliness, cleanliness and efficiency, the range of drink and/or food available and downright prejudice on the author's part, for which I make no apology.

No drink or favour was sought from any of the hostelries visited.

Time for a drink?

The current opening times are stated beside each pub's entry in this book. Most Edinburgh and Leith pubs are open for at least 12 hours per day. Many pubs take advantage of the enlightened licensing policy of the City Council and stay open almost every hour God sends, and more during the Festival.

Whose boozer is it anyway?

Managed	A pub owned and controlled directly by a large brewery or other company employing an in-house manager.
Free House	Used here to mean privately owned hostelries, though occassionally these can be grouped into small chains.
Chain	One of a group of pubs either commonly owned or 'themed'.
Franchise/Tenancy	These terms refer to brewery owned pubs which are leased to particular individuals rather than being directly managed.

What do you mean by that?

Blootered	An excess of joyousness, lurching towards incapacity.
Drinking Den	A hostelry with little or no style.
Fife	The country on the other side of the river Forth, which is north of the city. Known for unfathomable reasons as the Dark Kingdom. Natives known for wit and intelligence, or even low cunning.
Fifer	Someone from Fife, usually herein the Man from Fife.
Fleein	In a state of well-being brought on by alcohol.
Fou	A state just beyond fleein.
Fragile	A state of being not quite in attendance the morning after.
Gantry	The wall mounted repository for drink behind the bar.
Howff	A Scots word for a hostelry.
Listed	Buildings or fittings can be listed with government agencies to prevent them being tampered with or destroyed, This does not always work.
Mine Host	The manager or licencee of a given hostelry – of any gender.
Nip	A measure of spirits, now sadly decimalised and diminished.
Pick-up Joint	Place where members of different sexes, or the same sex, seek companionship and a cuddle.
Poser's Paradise	Hostelry where the clientele have a high opinion of themselves, even if no-one else has.
Roaring Fou	A state just before blootered.

THE ROYAL MILE

Edinburgh's Royal Mile stretches from Edinburgh Castle down to the royal residence of Holyroodhouse, and has been at the centre of Scotland's history for centuries. This is very much a tourist centre, with a varied mix of shops and a considerable range of pubs and restaurants. There are shops specialising in selling whisky, others that supply Highland dress and even one which is dedicated to art and craft work based on the art of the Picts – the tribal people who occupied much of Scotland in the Dark Ages. Some of the bars cater specifically to tourists, while others are local community bars. Nowadays, tourists visit Edinburgh all year round; the Hogmanay (New Year) celebrations recently have added another reason for visitors to come to Scotland's capital. Despite the sometimes almost overwhelming presence of visitors, the Royal Mile is a vital part of day-to-day Edinburgh; a city with a magnificent centre that is compact enough for people to walk just about everywhere. During the madness that is the Edinburgh Festival and Fringe, the Royal Mile is a constant outdoor theatre with all sorts of street performers and excerpts from current shows.

Ensign Ewart Lawnmarket *Free House*   A2

M-Th 11am-11.30pm, FS 11am-12am, Sun 12.30pm-12am
This is the nearest pub to Edinburgh Castle and is named after a young ensign who was a hero at Waterloo, having captured the standard of the French 45th Regiment. A large painting of this heroic episode hangs opposite the bar. Four real ales are available, as are a fine range of some three dozen malt whiskies, and not a bad pint of Guinness can be had too. Prices are no better than to be expected in this location. Food is available till 10.30 at night and fairly priced. It may be pub grub but it is fresh, well presented and worth the money. The military connection is long established, and forms a clear theme throughout the bar with sabres, bugles and muskets hanging from the rafters. There is a touch of Ye Olde English Pub in the rows of horse brasses nailed along the rafters. The historic feel to this bar is absolutely authentic. The original site, now in the cellars, dates back to 1603 at least – as is the case with many of the buildings on the Royal Mile, the present High Street being built over an earlier one. With candles on the tables, rough-cast walls and limited standing room at the bar, this is a comfortable howff which draws most of its custom from tourists, though there are locals who appear here on a regular basis. This is one of the glories of Edinburgh; even this close to the Castle itself, inhabitants still live in the heart of the city – a fact that constantly seems to surprise visitors from elsewhere in Britain. The Ensign Ewart has live traditional music most nights, and Sundays are particularly notable with the accordion wizard Sandy Brechin leading the fun. Amenities fine.

The Jolly Judge James Court *Free House*   A3

M-Th 11am-11pm, FS 11am-12am, Sun 12.30pm-11pm
This basement bar is up a close off the Royal Mile, in a location that is classic Edinburgh Old Town. Here you can sample two cask ales, around 30 malt whiskies, half a dozen wines and the usual suspects in other drinks. Prices are normal for this part of town which means a bit on the high side, and pub grub lunches are available from 12pm-2.30pm at reasonable prices. This very traditional looking, long, low bar room is in fact a recent addition. The roof is painted between the open rafters; a traditional 17th century Scottish touch in keeping with the age of the building

itself. Outside there are tables to sit at, on the off chance that
the sun shines in the summer. The crowd here is a mix of
tourists, students, MSPs and legal eagles. Amenities fine but
upstairs.

Deacon Brodie's Lawnmarket *Managed*   A4

10am-1am all week
This is a big, traditional style pub named after the Edinburgh
worthy who is said to have inspired Robert Louis Stevenson's
Jekyll and Hyde. By day he was a respectable member of the City
Council, and by night a devious burglar and robber, eventually
ending up on a gallows of his own design! Beer is all keg here
and a decent range of malts are on offer. Brodie's provides an
extensive range of food from its upstairs restaurant between
12pm-10pm and prices are not too bad considering the location.
It's position on Edinburgh's Royal Mile means that this is mainly
a tourist pub, though a few law professionals and people from
the new Scottish Parliament drop by. It tends to be steadily busy
at most times of the year and is always clean and well-kept. Good
amenities including a disabled toilet.

EH1 High Street *Free House*   A6

9am-1am all week
Despite the earlier disclaimers, a few café-bar type
establishments have managed to worm their way in and this is
one of them. With no real beers, EH1 has a wide range of bottled
beers and premium lagers on draft. Add to this cocktails,
pitchers, shooters and a substantial wine list, and the up market
intent is obvious. Coffee and food are available throughout the
day; mainly Scottish derived high class pub grub with lots of
salads (rabbit food muttered the Fifer). The decor is bright, light
and modern with an unusual steel bar and wrought ironwork on
the chairs. The clientele consists of tourists and law-types during
the day and a bit of a mix in the evenings. EH1 caters for a young
crowd at the weekends, and puts on DJs on Fridays and
Saturdays. Toilets fine but awkward for wheelchairs.

Fiscal and Firkin Hunter Square *Managed*   A7

M-Th 12pm-12am, FS 12pm-1am, Sun 12.30pm-12am
This is a completely new pub in a new building, that picks up on
some aspects of the traditional type approach. They have four
real beers, premium lagers, stouts and ciders and a range of
bottled beers and standard spirits. The wine list is good and well
priced. Prices are very good for this area, perhaps because of the

nearby backpackers' hostels. Food, cooked in-house with a vegetarian range and discounts for students, is available 12pm-10pm daily. The decor is a hotchpotch of barrels, sofas, tables, chairs and a pool table; the overall design is clearly by Job Lot. Aimed at the youth market, much of their trade comes from tourists. Friday nights they put on live blues. A light bright bar it does what it sets out to. Disabled toilets.

The Tron/It's A Scream Hunter Square *Chain*   A8

M-S 12pm-1am, Sun 12.30pm-1am
A massive bar on three levels, two of them below street level, this has recently become a theme pub based on a formula that has proved successful south of the border. Featuring reasonably priced premium lagers, trendy bottles and alcopops, with various offers for students, this is a youth theme pub. During the day only the top bar is open. The decor is bright, tongue-in-cheek Halloween and horror derived kitsch, with a touch of post-industrial design. Food, available till 7pm and cooked in their own kitchens, is unremarkable, and features all day breakfasts and Sizzler Specials; prices are fine. In the basement they hold Friday and Saturday discos playing what is known as 'cheesy' music. The Man from Fife said It's a Travesty, but it's youth-oriented policy seems to attract good custom. Disabled toilets on the ground floor.

The Mitre High Street *Managed*   A11

M-Th 11am-12am, FS 11am-1am, Sun 12.30pm-12am
A big bright and light pub with many traditional features, the Mitre has a range of keg beers and standard spirits that is pretty unremarkable. Food, which is mainly out of the freezer, is available from 12pm-10pm daily except Thursday, when it stops at 9pm for the Quiz. The bar itself has been redone so often that there is no sense of real continuity in an establishment that is recorded as having connections with Bishop Spottiswoode in the 15th century. What survives from Edwardian times is the original roof and a rather fine gantry. In the summer, with the big front windows open, it is a pleasant place to watch the world go by. Very much a tourist locale, there are strong rumours of ghosts in the cellar. Toilets fine but upstairs.

Royal Mile Tavern High Street *Managed*   A12

M-F 11am-12am, Sat 11am-1am, Sun 12pm-11pm
With up to five cask ales, over 80 malts and a fair wine list, this is a spanking clean and elegant bar. Featuring lots of wood

panelling with inset mirrors, good quality prints and a nice gantry, it retains some stained glass from earlier incarnations and is comfortable throughout. The back of the bar has a few booths and access to an upstairs non-smoking room, used for dining and functions. Food is all cooked in house and is good quality. A wide ranging menu specialises in mussels. Both drink and food are very well priced for a bar that has such an upmarket feel. Being on the Royal Mile, it does rely on the tourist trade and the staff claim to specialise in 'sparkling repartee with brilliant service'. As an ex rock 'n roll joint, it now possesses a different kind of charm. Toilets good and accessible.

The Tass Royal Mile/Jeffrey Street *Chain*   A13

M-Th 11am-12am, FS 12pm-1am, Sun 12.30pm-12am
This is a pub that unashamedly looks to exploit the reputation of our National Bard, Rabbie Burns. Named after one of his songs, the Silver Tassie, the pub boasts some interesting memorabilia like the collection of Burns china plates, though the statue of the bard himself will not be to everybody's taste. A medium sized boozer with three real ales, the Tass has its own kitchens downstairs and does traditional pub fare at reasonable prices. It actively encourages folk music sessions most nights, and is particularly busy during Edinburgh's Folk Festival round Easter time. Although attracting local musicians and singers to the sessions, the pub thrives on the tourist trade. Amenities are fine but there are stairs up to the ladies'.

The World's End High Street *Managed*   A14

M-S 11am-1am, Sun 12.30pm-1am
This low-roofed, dark and nookish bar might seem a little run down and kitsch with the combination of tartanry, wood panelling and rough stone walls. It has a couple of cask ales of supreme quality, a dozen malts and a couple of wines. The home-cooked food is standard fare (steak pie, haggis) but it was voted Best Pub Food in Edinburgh in 1998 which tells you something. They also cater for the vegetarian visitor and prices are very fair. These days the menu from World's End is pinned up in the coffee room of the temporary Scottish Parliament, which has to count as some sort of accolade. Named for its location in the Old Flodden Wall of Edinburgh, which was raised as a defensive structure against the English invasion of the 14th century, The World's End is a little piece of history. It is also very popular, with a steady trade of both regulars and tourists. It has been winning awards for years for its simple philosophy of good beer, good food and good service. The philosophy works. The decor consists of bits of

bric-a-brac and the odd print or ten, but nothing intrusive. The bar
is broken into small areas; the shape of the ancient building
demands it. This is a bar that claims regular customers from as
far off as Milton Keynes and Maidenhead; an English invasion
every couple of months that is welcome in these more peaceful
times. On Mondays and Thursdays live music is provided by a
singer-guitarist and tends towards folk and country. Awaiting
refurbishment as we go to print, we can only hope it doesn't
change too much. Amenities fine but the pub is entered up a
couple of stairs.

The Waverley St Mary's Street *Free House*   A15

M-S 11am-2.30am, Sun 5pm-12am
In a city like Edinburgh, famed throughout the world for the quality
of its pubs, the Waverley shows why. We need bars like the
Waverley to remind us that individuality is of prime importance.
This delightful spot in St Mary's Street, just off the Royal Mile, is
a smallish lounge-type pub with a large three sided bar, its back
against the front window. Immediately it becomes obvious there
is no television, no juke box or fruit machines. The walls have a
selection of prints and the roof is a riot of posters from
Edinburgh musical and theatrical productions over many years.
There are interesting plants, very fine decorated mirrors and a
small stuffed crocodile behind the bar. All beers are keg, but
there is a selection of over 70 malt whiskies. In the winter, food
is available at lunchtime and evenings, consisting of home-made
soup and toasted sandwiches. Prices are mid range for the area.
Upstairs there is a further room with a small bar that is open at
certain times. So far so good. However, what makes this place
so important is Ian's approach to running his pub. Sticking to old-
fashioned opening hours is the owner's prerogative, as is his
right to run the pub as he sees fit. The Waverley holds a very
important place in Scotland's cultural development over the past
thirty years. Upstairs was the location of a folk club in the 1960s
and 70s that helped further the careers of such luminaries as
Billy Connolly, Archie Fisher, the Clancy Brothers and Isla St Clair.
In more recent years, it has been the home of the Guid Crack
Club, an organisation at the heart of the recent development of
storytelling in Scotland that has served to breathe new life into
this traditional art form. Toilets fine, no disabled access.

White Horse Canongate *Tenancy*   A16

M-S 11am-11pm, Sun 12.30pm -11pm
With its unassuming frontage and traditional name, this is an
unusual High Street pub. Although it does attract tourists, it is

mainly a local pub and the smallest in the whole street. Beers are keg, but whisky is sold in 35 mls as opposed to 25, harking back to an old Scottish tradition! When I asked the staff about food I was told I could get crisps with a fork and knife! The locals have a fine sense of humour and are very welcoming – they say you don't have to be daft to drink here, but if you aren't you soon will be. This is the cheapest pub on the Royal Mile and has Country and western duos playing at the weekends. A regular told me it was a pub anybody's grandmother could safely drink in! The Man from Fife thought he was back home. Amenities fine and accessible.

Canons' Gait Canongate *Free House*   A17

MT 12pm-11pm, W 12pm-12.30am, Th 12pm-11pm, FS 11am-12am, Sun 12.30pm-11pm.
Although much is made of the Canon, with a large painting of him on the wall, he is historical tosh. The decor is unusual and individualistic, with some tartan and a lot of wood. The painted cupboards on the wall are particularly noticeable. Real beer is on offer, along with keg and a range of spirits. Food is cooked on the premises and lunch is available 12pm-3pm. There are plenty of seats and the menu changes regularly, unlike some of their competition! Like many of the nearby pubs, this is aimed at the tourist passing trade but they do hold an open mike comedy session downstairs every Wednesday night. There is a warm and quite friendly atmosphere, and the amenities are fine. With so much real history, why the Canon?

The Tolbooth Tavern Canongate *Tenancy*   A18

M-W 8am-11pm, Th-S 8am-12am, Sun 12.30pm-11pm
This comfortable little bar is open from early on for coffee and breakfasts, drawing its custom mainly from tourists with a sprinkling of regular locals. Although it looks very traditional – 18th century Scottish – this too is a refurbished hostelry with keg beers and the usual spirits. Food is all cooked on the premises and a function room upstairs does lunches. It has one traditional Scottish form of pub decoration over the bar, a collection of different kinds of whisky in miniature bottles – here for show not for tasting. Live music is put on every Saturday and tends towards pop songs of the past few decades. The ghosts here tend to knock things off walls, so beware. Disabled toilets are due to be installed soon.

Castle Bar Café Johnston Terrace *Chain*   A1

M-Th 12pm-12am, FS 12pm-1am, Sun 12.30pm-12am
Good food and good beer near the Castle, but the place still seems
cold and perhaps unsure of what it wants to be. Great balcony bar.

The Royal McGregor High Street *Free House*   A5

11am-1am all week
A long narrow lounge-type bar that caters to the tourists, it is
warm and comfortable without being in any way remarkable.

The Logie Baird High Street *Free House*   A10

9am-1am all week
A bar that is probably as much a restaurant, and although the
food is good it is a bit off-putting. Like an old fashioned railway
waiting room, somehow.

Jenny Ha's Canongate *Franchise*   A19

M-S 11am-11pm, Sun 12.30pm-11pm
A great big barn of a bar built in the 1960s, this is changing
hands and should become very successful once the new
Parliament is built (don't hold your breath).

Whistlebinkies South Bridge/Niddry Street *Free House* A9

7am-11pm all week
A real Edinburgh Jekyll and Hyde bar with both back alley and
main thoroughfare access to a pub with good music and a small
dance floor.

OLD TOWN

Edinburgh is a city that is divided into distinct areas. The Royal Mile itself runs through the Old Town, most of which is to the south of it. However in the wynds and closes to the north of the High Street there are some very interesting little areas – and pubs. This section covers the area between the Royal Mile and Waverley Station, incorporating Cockburn Street and Market Street, as well as Fleshmarket Close, so named for the meat market that used to be sited here. Fleshmarket Close has many steep stairs and it is suggested that it is approached with caution if several drinks have been taken. With the moving of the Scotsman newspaper offices, the likelihood of being knocked over by journalists stampeding towards Jinglin Geordie's or the Halfway House has thankfully passed. This area, with its high tenements and narrow wynds, is very atmospheric. Aside from pubs, the area also contains interesting shops and a range of restaurants of traditional Scottish style; Mexican, seafood, Greek. Well, Edinburgh does like you to think of it as cosmopolitan.

Scotsman's Lounge Cockburn Street *Free House*   **B1**

M-S 6pm-1am, Sun 12.30pm-1am

With keg beers and a standard range of spirits, the Scotsman's
Lounge is at first sight a bit intimidating. The decor has a
tendency towards being spartan and a little dingy at the same
time, but this is a veritable institution. Its long opening hours'are
of course a feature, but what makes this place unique is piping.
The juke box is nearly all pipe tunes and the pipe major courses
up at the Castle come in here to relax – if that is the right word.
They also put on live music every night of the week, with an
emphasis on folk music at weekends. So despite looking a little
tired and emotional, this is a magnet for tourists with lots of
backpackers among a steady regular crew. It is a magnet for shift
workers in the centre of the city. Look out for the important
Scottish historical documents on the walls, along with many
photographs of pipe major courses. The piping motif goes as far
as kilted dolls with bagpipes behind the bar, which are so horrible
they are funny. Although this is a pub which does not take itself
too seriously, after a couple of drinks it is easy to think that this
a little bit of Scotland that is already independent. A word of
warning – this is a pub with a lowish roof and if anybody takes
out a set of bagpipes, cover your ears. As our Man from Fife
says, the Highland bagpipes are best heard outdoors or in big
halls, not wee pubs. Toilets accessible.

Jinglin Geordie Fleshmarket Close *Free House*   **B2**

M-Th 11am-12am, FS 11am-1am, Sun variable

Recently refurbished, this bar down the narrow and steep
Fleshmarket Close serves only cask beers, has a range of 20
odd malt whiskies and the usual suspects in spirits. Food, which
consists of pies, toasties and snacks, is available all the time.
This L-shaped bar has long been known as a haunt of one of the
stranger sub-species of humans to be found in the Capital –
journalists. However the *Scotsman*, the once proud flagship of
the Scottish press, has moved from immediately next door and
this could change things. Whatever happens though, Jinglin's will
survive. This is because it has a steady regular trade of locals
and others from around the city. Fine modern stained glass
windows were put in as part of the recent refurbishment and the
short arm of the L-shape by the gas fire is a comfortable little
nook for couples – or as we Scots might say, it's like being at
your auntie's. This is not really true of the bar, where the
conversation can be of the barbed variety; and is none the worse
for that. Named after a phenomenally rich jeweller who became a

money lender to royalty in the 17th century (and a major philanthropist in the city), the atmosphere at Jinglin's tends towards the masculine and sporty, but women are always welcome. One anomaly the Man from Fife and I have long argued over is, why so many different deer antlers on the wall? One day we will ask Roger, mine host. This pub is not easily accessible to either wheelchairs or the less than mobile, a fact worsened by steps up into the bar.

Halfway House Fleshmarket Close *Free House* B3

M-Th 11am-11pm, FS 11am-1am, Sun 12.30pm-11pm
Two real ales, premium lager and a couple of dozen malts form the basis of the Halfway House's provision. They also stock a range of wines, in 14 bottles, called Minicellar which looks interesting. Food is restricted to sandwiches and filled rolls. This wee bar really is like someone's living room, with lamps and a few prints, and is kept spotless. Being only yards from the back door of Waverley Railway Station, they attract a lot of passing trade even if railway staff can no longer drop in for a pint in uniform. This is a quietish wee pub that is never actually empty, and over the years, like Jinglin's next door, became a bit of a press watering hole. They have a few regular customers and are popular with couples looking for a quiet corner. The amenities are accessible, but allow for the steepness of Fleshmarket Close.

McGuffie's/Doric Tavern Market Street *Free House* B4

M-Sat 11am-1am, Sun 12.30pm-1am
Here you have two pubs for the price of one. Downstairs is McGuffie's Tavern, while upstairs is the Doric, which includes restaurant service. McGuffie's has two cask ales and a dozen or so malts, while upstairs there are over 50 malts and an extensive wine list. The bar menu, which comes from the upstairs kitchen, is on from 12pm-6.30pm, while upstairs the a la carte selection is on till 10pm. Food prices are at a reasonable restaurant level for the quality, but the beer costs 20 pence more upstairs. The menu is Scottish based. Given its location, McGuffie's gets a mixed trade including the occasional hen party from Ireland, which can be fun. They are to be commended in having a children's licence till 6pm. At weekends, it can get very busy upstairs and down. Amenities fine and accessible.

The Hebrides Market Street *Free House*   B5

M-Th 11am-12am, FS 11am-1am, Sun 12.30pm-12am
This is often seen as a little piece of home transported from the
Outer Isles to the heart of the city; and not just because of the
name. On offer are one cask ale, a range of kegs and an
extensive selection of malts in the larger measure of 35 mls.
There is no food on offer, but the regulars will tell you to bring
your own grub in with you. A pub with no juke box or fruit
machines, and where the television only goes on on very special
occasions, this is one place to come to for the 'craic'. It is also
where pipe majors occasionally fall in, and the regular crowd are
friendly and welcoming to everyone. You do not have to speak
Gaelic to drink here! The decor is relatively undistinguished,
traditionally derived with a bit of tartan, and the best seats in the
house are at the bar. The visitors book says it all. One friendly
American wrote how wonderful it was to 'find ourselves in a
Smash Scottish Sitcom of Cheers.' Tourists are attracted in and
many come back, as do numerous flight crews, but given the
attendance of the regulars it is a puzzle as to how they can cater
for so many tourists! They also make a feature of postcards sent
from visitors who have returned home, showing just how
attractive traditional Scottish hospitality can be. Our Fife friend
resolved to visit the Outer Isles after one visit! Live Music –
Scottish of course – is on at night from Thursday through to
Sunday. Amenities are fine and accessible.

The Malt Shovel Cockburn Street *Managed*   B6

Sun-Th 11am-12am, FS 11am-1am
This is a large pub on two levels with areas separated by
dividers. It looks traditional, but even the imposing gantry and the
leaded glass are relatively new. Having undergone extensive
recent refurbishment (though there seem to be gaps in the back
room) the dark wood and the glass make it pretty much a cod-
Scottish traditional pub, with imitation shields and halberds and
other clichés on the walls. However, in other areas there is no
imitation. The six real ales and over a hundred malt whiskies
show this is a place where the serious drinker can relax (which
the Fifer did immediately on crossing the door – lifting him was
difficult). The prices are near the top end, though. With plenty of
seating, the Malt Shovel does a steady trade in food, which is
pretty standard brewery fare at medium range prices; the haggis
proves very popular. Grub is available from 12pm-6pm in the
week and till 3pm on a Friday. Saturdays and Sundays are for
drinking. They have quite a lot of regulars, who come here for the

beer, as well as lots of tourists and workers from the council buildings opposite. There is even a rumour that they will consider serving councillors. For many years the Malt Shovel has put on jazz on Tuesdays which is of the finest kind – swing a la Reinhardt-Grappelli. The band are called Swing 99, who I am sure I can recall as Swing 86, or was it 56? At the weekends the crowd is typically uptown and, like many other bars, during the Edinburgh Festival the pace is frenetic. Amenities are fine with disabled access.

Mary King's Tavern Cockburn Street *Managed*   B7

Sun-Th 5pm-12am, F 5pm-1am, Sat 12pm-1am
Very much a theme pub, this gothic boozer is named after Mary King's Close, now under the council buildings opposite, which had a particularly frightening ghost. With keg beers and only a handful of malt whiskies, they offer a range of cocktails and 'test tubes'; smaller versions of the same. Advertised on the wall are Seven Deadly Cocktails. Naturally, the decor is macabre kitsch with skeletons and skulls and other such gothic paraphernalia. Some of the devils – or are they imps? – are quite fun. The lighting is of course dark, which suits my Fife companion who is not that fond of daylight hours. This is a regular stop on city pub tours. The clientele includes local shopkeepers (Cockburn Street has long been a cool shopping street), shoppers and the odd vampire out on the town. Amenities are tolerable but the boys' room is down stairs.

Arcade Bar Cockburn Street *Free House*   B8

M-S 9am-1am, Sun 12.30pm-1am
Famous among city drinkers under a previous name, Jim's Inn, this was one of the first Edinburgh pubs to be allowed to open all day. Rumours abounded that the City Councillors chose the worst pubs for the all-day opening experiment so it would fail. The opposite happened and there are those that say this was brilliant double bluff. Before this bars closed from 2.30pm to 5pm which was a load of Puritanical tyranny! Anyway, nowadays the Arcade's a fine bright bar with an upstairs room mainly used for dining. The bar has two real beers, standard kegs, 15 malts and a good selection of wines. Food is available all day till nine at night, (12.30pm – 4pm on Sunday), cooked in their own kitchen and is very reasonable pub grub, ranging from breakfast to steaks. The actual bar is granite and the modern decor is both homely and comfortable. Amenities fine but all upstairs.

GRASSMARKET / TOLLCROSS

The Grassmarket has long been a part of Old Edinburgh that has an active social scene. Nowadays, it is very much a haunt of students and other young people at the weekends. This is a part of the town that thrives during the Festival and attracts tourists and revellers all the year round. A couple of the bars here tend towards the macabre, recalling the Grassmarket's role as the site of public hangings till the 19th Century. There are also many restaurants, delicatessens and bistros, and a range of interesting shops selling everything from antiques, to cheeses, to the remarkable brush shop – yes, there is a shop that sells just brushes in Victoria Street. Tollcross, once a village in its own right, is slightly further out past the Grassmarket and is a busy area, with the King's Theatre, a lot of shops and plenty of new housing going up apace. Very much a separate area, it contains some wonderful examples of Scottish pubs like Bennet's and the Golf Tavern. Between the Grassmarket and Tollcross there are some bars that have become strip show venues and are not really pubs any more.

Finnegan's Wake Victoria Street *Managed*　　　C1

M-S 12pm-1am, Sun 12.30pm -1am
If you have to have an Irish theme pub (and I remain to be convinced) this one will past muster. A vast barn of a place covered in an anarchic riot of posters and flags, this a real rarity – many Irish people living in Edinburgh drink here. Maybe something to do with TV coverage of Gaelic football on Sundays! There are the obligatory stouts and a range of keg beers with a selection of Irish and Scotch whiskies on offer. Food is never more than sandwiches but this place does a roaring trade. Why? Live music seven nights a week covering all kinds of folk-rock and modern traditionally derived music. It is fine place to hear music and attracts a range of customers from 18 to – if not 80, certainly well into their fifties. Amenities are good with disabled toilets.

The Bow Bar Victoria Street *Free House*　　　C2

M-S 11am-12.30am, Sunday 6pm-11pm
This is a traditional style stand up bar decorated in tasteful Victorian style, many of the old fittings being salvaged from the refurbishment of other pubs and it is hard to believe it is little more than a decade old. Previously a fifties stylistic horror, the Bow Bar has developed a loyal clientele and a substantial reputation. There are those who can wax as eloquently of cask conditioned ales as any connoisseur of wine and this is the place you can find them. With a run of eight real beers, with regular guests, all in excellent condition and supplied by air compressor pumps, this is a Mecca for the beer aficionado. Visitors should always remember that some of these beers are a little on the strong side and should be treated with respect. Food is limited to pies – traditionally the only food available in male only working men's Scottish boozers up to just a couple of decades ago. With the emphasis on the beer, the clientele is mostly male, and they draw people from a wide base. Lawyers from the nearby law courts can often be seen with clients of various descriptions. Odd university staff and students and a variety of locals all come to this watering hole, which also attracts substantial tourist trade. This is due in no small way to the fact that the Bow Bar appears in Good Beer guides throughout the world. Some also find their way here through its website. They also get a good selection of people wanting to sample their wide range of malt whiskies – sent in to sample the wares by specialist whisky outlets. The amenities are well up so standard and if this is your kind of pub, you won't get better.

The Last Drop Grassmarket *Managed*   C4

M-S 11am-1am, Sun 12.30pm-1am
The Last Drop is so named because it is opposite where public
hangings used to take place in Edinburgh up to the 19th Century.
However, any tendency to the macabre is avoided and the
traditional and slightly run down decor is offset by big welcoming
signs in many languages. This is a pub that actively wants the
young visitor trade and goes after it. They have no real beers, but
a pretty fair range of malt whiskies and an alright wine list.
Additionally, in the miserable Scottish weather, they do toddies
(hot whisky or rum with honey, cloves and lemon), mulled wines
and even hot port with spices! Table service is a nice touch and
food is cooked on the premises and served till 7.30pm. While
the menu is hardly exotic these days, there are quite substantial
student and backpacker discounts. While it is common for foreign
students to work in Edinburgh pubs – sometimes I think I am in
downtown Melbourne – the manager actively recruits his staff
from among the clientele. The bar is covered over with signed
foreign bank notes, many of which have been signed by series of
friends who have followed the route of earlier compatriots to
Edinburgh. This ensures lots of returnees and people who have
heard of the place by word of mouth. It also has ghosts in the
cellar, and it is a common occurrence for new staff to hear their
name being called when they are alone in the bar. Perhaps its an
internationally travelled ghost. The overall feel of the bar is
certainly young and friendly, and the Mad Fifer thought it a good
place to work on his Swedish, or was it Dutch? Amenities
adequate and accessible.

Maggie Dickson's Grassmarket *Managed*   C3

11am-1am all week
While next door The Last Drop does not pick up on the macabre
history of the Grassmarket, Maggie Dickson's certainly does. The
bar is named after a fish seller who was convicted under the
disgraceful Concealment of Pregnancy Act of 1690. Her baby died
just after birth and was found by the river Tweed where the
distraught Maggie had left it; she was hanged in the Grassmarket
in 1742. A popular and well known woman, her execution
attracted thousands. Her body was saved by the crowd from
medical students trying to take the corpse for experiments, after
a great scuffle. Her friends wanted to give her a decent burial in
her native Musselburgh, and just as she was about to be buried,
noises were heard from within the coffin. At once the coffin was
opened and Maggie was found alive! She lived for another 40

years, known by one and all as Half-Hangit Maggie. This dark and almost gloomy pub has a decor all its own. Half way down the bar there is a skeleton in a glass coffin hanging from the ceiling while posters of Nosferatu and other horror films vie with handcuffs and stories of grisly crimes on the walls. A mummy is present along with a few other plastic skeletons. These are interspersed with such totally incongruous objects as ski sticks and kayak paddles. There is a strong Gothic feel to the fittings and upholstery and the whole affair is quite gloriously tongue in cheek. Beers are all keg and there is a decent if limited range of malt whiskies. Cocktails are on offer, with 'test-tube' miniatures at £1. Food is brought in pub grub and prices are standard for the area. Amenities accessible.

White Hart Grassmarket *Managed* C5

M-W 11am-12am, Th-S 11am-1am, Sun 12.30pm-12am
One of the oldest pubs in the centre of the town, the White Hart has been reworked but is still relatively small. The decor is standard traditional and they have a couple of real beers on tap. They stock a dozen malt whiskies, but no wine list to talk of. Food is pretty much big sandwiches and standard freezer fare with the exception of daily home-made soup; prices are decent. These days they have music on about once a fortnight and it tends towards the folky. They also stage quizzes and plan something called a play-station league – for people younger than your correspondent, I presume. While they get the usual weekend throngs, during the week the pub is frequented by a mix of ages and types, and during the summer a lot of tourists. Amenities adequate and accessible.

Beehive Inn Grassmarket *Managed* C6

M-Th 11am-12am, FS 11am-1am, Sun 11am-10pm
This big three roomed bar in a traditional style was once one of the country's finest real ale houses. Nowadays it has three cask conditioned beers, half a dozen malts and a shortish wine list, in addition to a standard range of spirits and bottled beers. Upstairs there is a restaurant which also supplies food to the bar from noon till 10pm. One room is non-smoking for diners. The restaurant has an à la carte menu, so the bar food is on the high-class side, but fairly priced, as is the drink. With old Edinburgh prints, cases of spigots and other brewing paraphernalia on the walls, this is a slightly run-down pub with a traditional ambience. With numerous ghosts said to inhabit the basement, it is the starting point of some of Edinburgh's Guided Pub Tours. Very busy at the weekends. Toilets fine but up some stairs.

Fiddler's Grassmarket *Tenancy*   **C7**

M-Th 11am-12am, FS 11am-1am, Sun 12.30pm-12am
For long a Scottish & Newcastle managed house this is a good-going traditional type hostelry that has lately been in need of a bit of refurbishment. The gantry, with its notable clock, is an original Victorian feature and old fiddles feature strongly in the decor. With a couple of real ales and a standard provision of spirits, the Fiddler's does not provide food. There are lots of 'entertainment' machines in the bar and back room, and games of dominoes are a regular occurrence. Once a month they put on a karaoke night and the long standing tradition of folk music sessions continues on Monday nights. The customers are mainly regulars who live nearby, and during the summer and the Edinburgh Festival it has a steady stream of visitors. It is a comfortable place to drink but is nothing out of the ordinary. Toilets are down very steep stairs.

The Soupdragon West Port *Tenancy*   **C8**

12pm-1am all week, open for Sunday breakfasts 12pm-3pm
Another pub that has begun to feature food, even so far as to put it in its name, is the Soupdragon. They really do place an emphasis on food, with an extensive menu that sees standards like haggis, neeps and tatties alongside deep-fried brie. It has one cask ale, a range of keg beers, 5 malt whiskies, six wines and all the standard bottles and sprits. Prices for drinks are standard for the area, but the food is definitely good value and all cooked in-house. They get a lot of custom from the nearby art college, and a range of office workers and tourists. The staff say there's a different crowd every night, though they do have a few regular locals. Their downstairs bar has jazz on a Monday and DJs at the weekends. Amenities fine and accessible.

The Blue Blazer Spittal Street *Franchise*   **C13**

M-W 11am-11pm, Th 11am-12am, FS 11am-1am, Sun 12.30pm-11pm
Yet another traditional ale house, the Blazer has six or seven cask ales, a couple of dozen malts, half a dozen wines and all the usual suspects. Known as a real beer pub, they only have snacks available at the moment but aspire to greater things soon. The designers have gone for an authentic bar feel with the wooden floor, pews and old Edinburgh prints on the walls. Some original features like the roof and a fireplace have been retained. A two-roomed bar, the Blazer has a mixed bag of customers – a

considerable number of local regulars, a steady passing trade and a few theatrical types too; the Lyceum Theatre is just around the corner. A comfortable if unremarkable spot for good beer. Toilets fine but downstairs.

The Hogshead Spittal Street *Managed*   C14

11am-1am all week, open for Sunday breakfast

This is a great barn of a pub converted from an old warehouse. Part of a chain of pubs modelled on traditional lines by one of the big breweries, they try to provide choice. With up to 16 cask ales at a time, one of the notorious cask conditioned ciders, premium lagers, 18 malt whiskies, as many wines, a couple of champagnes, a collection of Belgian beers and all the trendy drinks you can think of, they succeed. Chuck in jugs of beer, pitchers and shooters and you really are spoiled for choice. Prices are very good and they usually have one or two special promotions on. The pub, which has lots of tables and a raised dining area at the rear, has an extensive and varied menu at reasonable prices, which is available till late in the evening. With such a choice, it is not surprising that they get a lot of custom across a very wide range. Here you will find groups of students, local shopkeepers lunching or unwinding after a day's work, business suits and older women, who come in to sample the odd glass of wine, or six. This is a place for meeting people and for partying, and at the weekends it fills up with a dedicated crowd of pleasure-seekers. Perhaps trying too hard to be all things to all people, the Hogshead just about pulls it off. The Man from Fife wanted to try all of the cask ales on offer so we had to make our excuses and leave. Big Ian, standing at the bar, said 'Haste ye back', which from an Englishman was very odd. Amenities fine and accessible.

Cloisters Brougham St *Chain*   C16

M-Th 11am-12am, FS 11am-12.30am, Sun 12pm-12am

This is a converted manse – the Scots word for the house of a minister, usually, like this one, next door to the relevant church. What previous incumbents of this 19th Century building would think of it now being a pub might be interesting – for every Church of Scotland minister who would rail against the evils of the demon drink, there would always be another who liked the odd bucket or two of claret or was involved in the manufacture and distribution of illegally made whisky. Truly, Scottish drinking has a chequered history, and such ambivalent attitudes are part of our national psyche – both of them! Cloisters is a clean airy place with up to nine real ales at a time and a list of over 50

malt whiskies. There are echoes of the ecclesiastical in the decor
with pew-type benches and even in the square-shaped bar and its
chunky gantry. There are half a dozen wines on offer and lunch is
available from 12pm-3pm daily. All cooked in house, it is the
standard pub grub with variations, including vegetarian dishes.
This is clearly a beer shop and attracts a clientele that includes
students, local professional people and regulars from around the
city who appreciate the beer. There is no entertainment of any
kind including canned music, and the atmosphere encourages
conversation – calling it a hallowed hall for drinking might not be
going too far! The big fire, though imitation coal gas, gives a focal
point. All in all a very pleasant place to concentrate on matters in
hand – beer. Toilets fine but down stairs.

The International Bar Brougham Place *Free House*   C17

M-S 9am-1am, Sun 12.30pm-1am
This is a long narrow bar that serves four cask ales, 12 malts
and a fair range of bottled beer and other spirits. It has some
fittings dating from the beginning of the century, such as the
ceiling and cornices and the stained glass window at the rear,
which is particularly fine. This is a bar where food is not a priority,
but toasties and rolls are always to be had. The gantry is modern
but the feel of the place is very much that of a long-term local
community bar. Apart from their steady regulars, they have some
passing trade from the nearby King's Theatre and from people
walking in the Meadows. They have no entertainment, no darts or
dominoes or board games. Although understated and on the quiet
side, the regulars think this is one of Edinburgh's best pubs,
which tells you all you need to know. Amenities fine but no
wheelchair access.

Bennet's Leven Street *Managed*   C18

M-W 11am-11.30pm, Th-S 11am-12.30am, Sun 12.30pm-11pm
Although no longer privately owned and now under the direct
control of Scottish & Newcastle, this remains one of the finest
pubs on the planet. They have two cask ales and in excess of a
hundred malt whiskies. The beer has changed from earlier times,
but is still very fairly priced and the decor of this magnificent
Victorian bar has remained intact – the entire bar is listed. The
fine exterior which features superb leaded glass is matched
inside with a veritable cornucopia of architectural delights (and I
am writing this sober). The lovely long bar with its original tiered
and alcoved gantry housing the whisky collection, has a wee snug
bar at the end beside the door, separated by a wooden and
leaded glass panel. This was a common feature in Scottish bars

where women, or men who didn't want to be seen, could be
served in some privacy. The bar retains original working brass
water taps and on the gantry is a brass gas cigarette lighter that
used to be fitted beside the snug. Opposite the bar there is a
series of mirrors surrounded by decorated tiles and carved
wooden pillars behind fitted seats. The small tables are
replacements of earlier ones with glass covered maps on their
tops. Food is available from 12pm-3pm and 5pm-8pm featuring
pies and roast meats, chicken and pasta at reasonable prices.
Bennet's attracts a totally mixed crowd of suits and students,
shoppers and scribes, male and female and a regular influx at
intervals from the King's Theatre next door. Through the back is
another bar named the Green Room, and the corridor through to
it has an interesting recent mural. The amenities are fine with a
step up to the ladies. Wonderful timeless atmosphere.

The Auld Toll Bar Leven Street *Managed*   C19

Sun,M 11-11, TW 11-11.30, Th-S 11-1
This fine two roomed local community bar has three cask ales
and 30 malts, all of which are very reasonably priced. Food is
restricted to snacks and toasties. With a lovely big gantry and
some interesting panelling and other Edwardian features, this is
a big bright bar with seats at the bar and round the walls. There
is an interesting second room round the other side of the bar,
decorated with old music hall posters and other theatrical
paraphernalia. Very much a pub for regulars, many of whom come
from nearby, they also draw in some students as there are a lot
of large flats in the area which attract these creatures. Theatre-
goers from the King's just down the road drop in too. A steady
community style pub, this has long had a fine reputation and is
very much a middle of the road pub. Disabled access to the
amenities.

The Belfry Bar Bruntsfield Place *Free House*   C20

M-W 11am-12am, Th-S 11am-12.30am, Sun 12.30pm-12am
Some pubs just make you laugh – in the nicest possible way of
course, and this is one of them. A bright very modern looking
long bar with a fine wooden floor and a beer garden out the back,
this pub takes its name seriously. There are plenty of bats in this
belfry. The decor features an abundance of them and the
interesting use of candles and mirrors make for a memorably
decorated howff. With two or three cask ales always on, a dozen
malts, six wines and some cocktails, this is a bar that gives
choice. Food is on from 12pm-9pm including breakfasts. Drinks
are slightly expensive. A mixed clientele in the daytime, it is a

student hang-out in the evenings and weekends, but don't let that put you off! This is a pub worth looking into. Disabled access to the toilets which have a nice line in cartoons.

The Golf Tavern Wright's Houses *Managed*   C21

Sun-Th 12pm-12am, FS 12pm-1am
This is an old pub that has been a licensed premises since the middle of the 18th Century. Its location overlooking Bruntsfield Links gives it its name. The 18th Century poet Allan Ramsay wrote, 'When we were wearied at the gowff/ Then Maggie Johnson's was our howff' – referring to the landlady of his time and the custom of playing golf, which as everyone knows is a purely Scottish invention. Surfing was never a possibility. Even today if you want you can borrow clubs from the pub and have a go at the short hole course on the Links. The bar itself is a large area with a pillared off section opposite. They have at least four cask ales and a dozen malts at a time but do not favour cocktails. Food, which is mainly frozen stuff, is available from 12pm -7pm and reasonably priced, while the drink is on the expensive side. The entirety of this pub is protected by being listed and has an interesting big gantry and some fine leaded glass features. The pub also contains a handful of motifs relating to golf, a Scottish invention of course. This is mainly a student pub, but the staff maintain it is not a cattlemarket (a place where people seek out members of the opposite sex) and it attracts a few older regulars among whom there are many couples. Like other places that tend towards sophistication, they provide a good selection of newspapers on the bar. A big bonny bar that is well worth a visit whether or not you like golf. Disabled access to the acceptable amenities.

Jackson's Bar Lady Lawson Street *Free House*   C9

M-S 12pm-1am, Sun 12.30pm-1am
A newish long bar of a pub with a good line in real beer that caters mainly for regulars and the Art College at the top of the street. Friendly and welcoming.

The Cas Rock West Port *Tenancy*   C10

M-Th 12pm-12am, F 12pm-1am, S-Sun 12.30pm-1am
A pub that has live music on most nights show-piecing local, and generally young talent. The music has a slight tendency to loudness.

The Western Bar West Port *Free House* C11

M-Th 12pm-12am, FS 12pm-1am, Sun 12.30pm-12am
The first pub to have go-go dancers, this one has not gone the
way of its fellows and encompassed lap-dancing; it sticks to what
it knows best.

Burke and Hare West Port *Free House* C12

1pm-1am all week
Once a great rock 'n' roll and bikers' bar, now sadly a place that
puts on strippers and lap-dancers, among other sleazy
attractions. Don't take your granny here.

The Illicit Still Bread Street *Tenancy* C15

M-S 12pm-1am, Sun 2pm-1am
Busy and welcoming wee pub in a newish building that seems to
cater for a regular set of customers so it already has a good
atmosphere.

AROUND THE COWGATE

The Cowgate runs under George IV Bridge and the North Bridge, from the Grassmarket down to Holyrood Palace and the site of the new Scottish Parliament. In recent years this area has seen considerable redevelopment, with new court buildings and a plethora of new pubs. With buildings rising well over a hundred feet (30 metres) on both sides the Cowgate can be a bit gloomy, but these days it has all sorts of attractions along its length, particularly near the university. Several pubs off the street itself have been included. This is an area where bars open late and the dedicated drinker, or late night worker, can find drinking company through the night. Some of the bars here are dingy, downmarket and bordering on the sleazy, while others pride themselves on being at the cutting edge of trendiness. One old watering hole of much fame, the Green Tree, is even as we go to print rising like a phoenix into something spanking new for the millennium. Others, like Sneeky Pete's, are pretty much as they have been for years. The area throbs at the weekends and is a total madhouse of late night comedy – professional and unintended – during the Festival. The Cowgate is Edinburgh's Underworld, but comparisons with Bladerunner locations are entirely fanciful, aren't they?

Oz Bar Candlemaker Row *Free House*   D1

M-Th 12pm-1am, FS 12pm-2am, Sun 12.30pm-1am
Just to show a bad idea is not limited to breweries, this free
house has gone for the Australian theme. It shouldn't be
confused with Bar Oz in Forrest Road – though how you can tell
them apart might not be too clear after a few tubes, Mate.
Actually this is a place where lots of Antipodeans do hang out,
even if its designer based his idea of Australia on Hollywood –
ergo the corrugated iron frill over the bar. Here they have Fosters
on draught and other keg beers, a lot of Down Under bottles, the
usual spirits and jugs of beer. A biggish, bright and airy pub, this
one does show a little wit. The menu is Australia shaped, and
features the aptly named Skippyburger, made with kangaroo
meat, and of course kangaroo pie! Snags (sausages) and prawns
are also available and the general Surf's Up theme is all too
evident. Priced towards the high side, it is a fine place when the
sun shines and the big windows are opened to let the car fumes
in. It is popular with students, backpackers – there are a couple
of backpacker hostels nearby – and other tourists; it also gets a
regular crew of a few locals. This is probably because they
appreciate an ambience that the staff describe as having 'the
odd bit of serious drinking' going on. They always have drinks
promotions and make a feature of Aussie sport on the Big
Screen; which is great if you like rules, Mate. In true role reversal
style, all the bar staff are Scots. Nae Worries, Jimmy. Toilets
decent and accessible.

The Three Sisters Cowgate *Free House*   D3

M-S 9am-1am, Sun 12.30pm-1am
This monstrosity of a bar is actually three in one; hence the
name. Undoubtedly the place everyone is talking about, the
takings here are legendary. They have a couple of real ales in
decent condition, all the premium lager you could want and trendy
beers, alcopops, cocktails in shooters and pitchers, all at top end
prices. Food is available all day till ten at night and the menu is
extensive; everything is created in the kitchens and is not
horrendously priced. The design concept – and whatever the
designer was drinking at the time I want nothing to do with – is
supposedly an American bar, a Gothic bar and an Irish bar. Our
Fife friend said it was a dog's breakfast. The American bar is
light, bright, with lots of wrought iron and a plain bar. The Gothic
bar reminded the Fifer of a brothel he saw in a film; the booths
with doors are noticeable. The Irish bar at the back is over-
designed but strangely comfortable after a few pints. With up to

40 staff on at the weekends, there are mutterings around the
town of people being unable to get a drink at all, such are the
crowds at weekends in particular. They have to be commended
on having a children's licence, and their policy of showing films
on a wall in their outdoor seating area is original. They have a
variety of DJs on throughout the week and they do try to keep a
buzz going. Such is the fame (or notoriety) of the place that you
always find more than just students and young trendies about the
place. They have disabled amenities but lack enough toilets for
the crowds they get. Still, they are trying, but this is primarily a
cash cow.

The Living Room Cowgate *Managed*   D5

M-S 12pm-1am, Sun 12.30pm-12.30am
Even with three cask ales, premium lagers, a decent range of
malts and pitchers of cocktails at reasonable prices, this is a
place that only really breathes at night time. There are sofas in
the back bar which make it a little homely, but the general decor
is rough cast walls with prints and posters. Food is cheap,
available from 12pm-6pm, good value and cooked in house.
Another bar with DJs, on Wednesdays and Saturdays, they cater
for a party crowd with no real regulars and are very much part of
the Cowgate scene – don't take your granny here. This is another
pub that doubles as an avenue for comedy in the Festival, though
the young crowd that pack the place out every weekend create
their own laughs. The words cattle and market spring to mind.
They have disabled toilets.

Bliss Cowgate *Managed*   D6

1pm-1am all week
This trendy bar is owned by Belhaven Breweries who are clearly
going for the youth market with this modern, post industrial bar
(service pipes in the open and so on). The name is not exactly
subtle either. It is, nonetheless, plush and decent sized: the
mottled paint-work and interesting lighting are worth noting, and
there is the usual wrought iron effect furniture about. With keg
beers, shooters, pitchers and an ever changing array of chic
bottled drinks, prices are high – but they do have extensive happy
hours and lots of promotions. No food is available other than
snacks. They put on DJs on Thursday, Friday and Saturday nights
with a range of music from R 'n' B to house. Not the place for a
contemplative real beer freak, then, but they do seem to have got
their target market pretty sussed. Toilets fine and disabled
friendly.

Bannerman's Cowgate *Chain*   D7

M-Th 5pm-1am, F-Sun 9am-1am
This is a striking if slightly run down pub. Set in the vaulted
cellars of an original Edinburgh tenement – try looking up and
counting how many storeys there are in the building when you
leave – it is a bit like a central European bar; you can imagine
Harry Lime drinking here. Not much can be done to the decor
with only the stone roofs and walls of the original cellars to work
on, and there is a touch of the macabre in the various spaces
and rooms off the bar. With three cask ales, a plethora of malt
whisky, the usual kegs and spirits, the prices here are, like most
of the Cowgate, on the high side. Food is available till 10pm, all
cooked on the premises, and they open early on Sundays for
breakfasts – which are also available on Saturdays. On
Wednesdays and Sundays they have indie rock bands playing,
while Thursday, Friday and Saturday they have DJs, with an
inclination towards the cheesy. It is good to see someone at
least giving space to both live music and DJ sounds. On Tuesday
they throw taste out of the window for a karaoke night, and on
Mondays they host a Comedy Quiz. This commitment to
entertainment means that this traditional folk pub of yore now
has a younger, trendier clientele, and weekends are frenetic. Its
setting lends it an atmosphere at once sophisticated and a little
bit sleazy – in the best possible taste of course. Amenities fine
but no disabled toilets.

Holyrood Tavern Cowgate *Free House*   D12

M-S 12pm-12.45am, Sun 12.30pm-12.45am
With six cask conditioned ales, 15 malt whiskies, a good range of
blended whiskies, and many other spirits, there is much here for
the discerning drinker. Included is cask conditioned cider – a
suspiciously pleasant tasting beverage that can affect one's
balance in a sneaky fashion! Treat this one with caution! Food is
available from 12pm-2pm and 5.30pm-8pm and like the drink is
reasonably priced for the area. This is a big traditional style bar
with rooms going off it, lots of wood panelling and pub mirrors.
There is plenty of comfortable seating and while quiet during the
week, it fills up at weekends with students and other young
people. They have a dart board, an eclectic juke box, and the
staff proudly claim, 'this is a pub, not a theme bar'. Nuff said.
Disabled toilets.

Royal Oak Infirmary Street *Tenancy*   D10

M-S 9am-2am, Sun 12.30pm-2am
This is an Edinburgh institution with an upstairs and downstairs
bar; it has been the centre of much musical activity down the
years. With two cask ales, a wide selection of malts and blended
whiskies, this is a pub where musicians often gather after playing
elsewhere. Although predominantly a folk music hangout, other
types of music occasionally erupt in the sessions that take place
here. It has been a pub for over a century and a half. Upstairs is
a smallish square bar with an Edwardian gantry that is brightly lit
and has lots of standing room. Downstairs there is a cellar type
lounge with more seating than standing room. The only things
available to eat here are crisps and nuts – this is a place for
carousing and singing. The upstairs bar has music every night,
and downstairs on Thursdays, Fridays and Saturdays.

No. 1 Cellar Bar Chambers Street *Free House*   D11

M-S 12pm-1am, Sun 6pm-1am
This basement bar, which opens till 3am during the Festival, is a
typical jazz cellar. With a couple of cask ales, a decent wine list
and a range of cocktails at mid range city centre prices, this is a
place for the hep cat. The wood panelled, long curved room has
photographs of jazz performers and interesting stuff, like framed
bits of wine cases. The bar itself is smallish, with tables and
chairs laid out at the far end in cabaret style. Food consists
solely of filled rolls. The theme of the place is definitely jazz.
There is live music, with no cover charge, from Wednesdays to
Saturdays with a range of styles featured. With a happy hour from
4pm-8pm, they attract a mix of customers and have a steady
trade during the day with the cool cats arriving later. Amenities
fine.

The Subway Cowgate *Free House*   D2

9pm-3am all week
Long a late-night time haunt for those who like the wild side of
life, it sees no need to compromise its mission whatsoever – and
that's just fine.

The City Café Blair Street *Free House*   D4

11am-1am all week
I am unsure of whether this is café-bar or a bar-café, but the
atmosphere seems oddly sophisticated and cosmopolitan.

Doctor Watt's Library Bar Robertson's Close *Free House*   **D9**

> 11am-1am all week
> Overlooking the Cowgate, this student bar deserves a dug or three
> for its name alone. Gives 'I'm off to the Library' a new twist!

Black Bo's Bar Blackfriars Street *Free House*   **D8**

> Bar 4.30pm-1am Restaurant 6pm-10.30pm
> Another fine establishment going along with the increasing trend
> of bars being restaurants and restaurants being bars.

UNIVERSITY AREA

What is about students? They might have lost the radical edge that older generations remember with such fond memories, but their dedication to the pursuit of hedonism continues unabated. I suppose you are only as old as you feel, though, as several roués of my acquaintance in their 50s and 60s still maintain. This accounts for the diversity of pubs and bars around the University area that thrive on the student trade. It has also been known for lecturers to take the odd half pint shandy; though the famed madmen of yesteryear seem thin on the ground now. The route you will follow if you take these pubs in order will let you sidle round the edge of the University sampling a truly wondrous selection of drinking dens from the plain and ordinary to the plain daft.

Scruffy Murphy's George IV Bridge *Managed*   E2

M-S 11am-1am, Sun 12.30pm-1am
This is one of the plague of Irish theme pubs that have so excited the breweries while leaving so many of their customers unimpressed. Having removed a fine old bar, the brewers then put in this riot of wood with such subtle touches as signs in Irish, a different name for the room off the bar and a load of pseudo Irish tat. Both food and drink are relatively standard, though not

cheap, and though the staff are friendly and efficient there is no escaping the feeling that this type of pub is on the way out. They put on Irish folk music on Saturday nights which is a bit off when Scottish music is every bit as good. I have had a decent breakfast here though the Man from Fife simply says Bah Humbug. Toilets down stairs.

Greyfriars Bobby Candlemaker Row *Managed*   E3

M-S 11am-12.30am, Sun 12.30pm-1am

This smallish pub with its imposing, and rather English looking frontage, is named after a piece of romantic Edinburgh history. A wee Highland Terrier, Greyfriars Bobby, features in a tale of devotion where the dog sat by its master's grave in Greyfriars Kirkyard, behind the pub, for 14 years after his death till its own demise. A statue of the dog is on a plinth at the end of the railings opposite the pub. Cynics have suggested this vigil took place at the wrong grave but the tale travelled as far as Hollywood, guaranteeing an ongoing stream of tourists coming to visit the nice wee dog. Greyfriars Kirkyard is itself worth a visit, being the last resting place of many of the city's notable citizens down the centuries. The bar is mock Victorian though some of the wooden fittings are original and worth a look. The genuine stuff here predates the recent fad for false Victoriana that has ruined so many real traditional pubs in the town. Both drink and food are pretty standard fare and tend towards the upper price range. Meals are served from 12pm-8pm and are cooked on the premises. There are some interesting prints of old Edinburgh on the wall but nowadays this is all too common. This is a common meeting place for young people at the weekends intent on sampling the delights of a few of the city's many licensed hostelries – or going on a pub crawl if you want to be crude. The clientele is a mix of tourists, a few students, the odd local and some passing trade. Business is steady throughout the week and The Bobby, as it has long been known, has no problem holding its own against modern themed bars in the area. Amenities are fine.

Sandy Bell's Forrest Road *Managed*   E4

M-S 11am-1am, Sun 12.30pm-11am

This Scottish & Newcastle managed pub is at first sight kind of drab. It has no particular architectural merit, though the gantry is quite pleasant. Bell's is quite small, serves no food and dropping in during the day you might think this is just a quiet local boozer with a smattering of students, where nothing much happens. You would be wrong. This pub has been known to aficionados of traditional music throughout the world for the past thirty years and more. Situated close to the university, long ago it became the watering hole for academics and students from the School of Scottish Studies, ensuring a regular stream of storytellers, singers, folklorists and musicians coming through its doors to augment the local musicians and singers. At one time (far off in the murky drink-bedimmed past) instruments were frowned upon, singing was the thing. Nowadays, singing is itself rare and the nightly sessions are primarily instrumental. Several now well-known bands and musicians started out in Bell's, and it is always a possibility that some or other of the bigger names in Scottish traditional music will turn up. Visiting musicians, dropping in to play from Ireland and North America in particular, are a regular feature. Bell's does have a regular local daytime and night time clientele but it is the music that gives the place its attraction. The bar staff have developed a fine line in dismissive patter but don't let this fool you. Charlie and his staff are as irascible as they pretend (not)! The amenities are basic, and can be awkward to get to if there's a big session on but this is part of the charm of the place so people tend not to care – they are there for the music.

Bar Oz Forrest Road *Managed*   E5

M-S 12pm-1am, Sun 12.30pm-1am
We've had a rash of Irish pubs: are we now about to see a plague of Ozzie boozers? This massive converted Masonic hall has a large central bar and a balcony with lots of seating. The beer is all keg, there are lots of types of bottled beers, jugs are available and wine comes in two colours. Food is surprisingly cooked in house and perfectly acceptable at very good prices – available 12pm-9pm. This is obviously a student bar but the designer needs shooting. What exactly has a corrugated iron strip over the bar pretending to be a roof really got to say? As original and authentic as an Irish theme bar, with such subtleties as signs giving the distance to Sydney and Melbourne, I was never in an Australian boozer remotely like this. Still, bright and breezy, commercially calculated and no doubt guaranteed to do business. Disabled access and toilets.

Bar Iguana Lothian Street *Chain*   E8

9am-1am All week, food 9am-10pm
Bar Iguana is one of those modern café-style bars that are beginning to appear, but is quite distinctive for its type. The decor is light and bright with stone flagged and wooden flooring and an airy atmosphere. Bar Iguana sees itself as an 'in, happening kind

of place'. A group of four TV screens was showing an episode of the Simpsons on my last visit. With no real beers but a range of (expensive) premium draught lagers and beers and a wide variety of bottled beers, they are catering for a young and well-off clientele. There is a pretty decent wine list – and no surprise in them stocking four kinds of Champagne. They also have enough spirits to cater for a range of cocktails and have a policy of keeping up with what is new on the booze front. Food is modern, trendy and is available along with coffee from nine in the morning. Staff told me the place is a bit Jekyll and Hyde – the day mix of students, lecturers, medical staff and suits being replaced at nights with a younger, groovier mix of people. Which is the Jekyll, which the Hyde? The clientele at nights and at weekends is basically under 30, and the atmosphere is very clubby. Five nights of the week Bar Iguana has resident DJs playing to a variety of tastes, including drum 'n' bass, hip-hop, house, jungle and funk with a touch of future jazz and Latin grooves. In other words, an eclectic mix of dance-club beats for the cognoscenti. One interesting innovation is 'lager miles' – they are the first pub we have heard of with customer cards – points awarded going towards holidays booked through a travel agent. Amenities are clean, efficient and accessible. Worth its rating in its utter determination to servicing its own market.

The Captain's Bar College Street *Tenancy*   E9

M-Th 11am-11pm, FS 11am-12am, Sun 12.30pm-11pm
This tenanted pub is a small traditional stand up bar tucked in behind the Old Quad of Edinburgh University. One of the few city centre pubs that still looks pretty much as it started out a century ago, it is clean and well-kept. Almost always busy, The Captain's has a couple of real ales along with a standard selection of whiskies. Food is limited to snacks. The traditional gantry has a few items of real original bar ephemera. The clientele are mainly local working people and few students drop in, though university academic and administrative staff sometimes do. This an active social club and the bar has a small library, charging a fee which goes to charity. Despite the ghost of the old Captain himself in the cellar this is a friendly and welcoming place that is a fine example of a traditional Scottish city pub. Amenities OK.

The Woolpack Potterow *Chain*   E12

M-S 11am-1am, Sun 12.30pm-1am
This big, new, traditionally inspired pub adjoining the University takes the name of an old pub destroyed in Edinburgh University's

vandal period of the late 1960s. The mainly wooden decor and massive central bar are light coloured and the imitation original artworks on the wall could be worse. It has a handful of real ales and a very good selection of malt whiskies. All food is made on the premises and is good quality standard pub fare aimed unashamedly at the student market. With its coal fire, selection of newspapers and friendly staff, it is a comfortable shop that picks up at nights and the weekends, particularly with the Friday night DJ. Other than students the clientele consists of University staff, some medics and office staff. The man from Fife reckons it is efficient rather than attractive. Prices pretty standard. Disabled toilets.

The Pear Tree West Nicolson Street *Free House*   E13

M-W 11am-12am, Th-S 11am-1am, Sun 12.30pm-1am
Set in the historic Pear Tree House, this is an interesting and lively pub. The bar itself is a squarish room with a central bar and chairs and tables round the walls. These days they have no real ales, but stock a wide range of keg and bottled beers. Food is served till 3pm and is of the buffet type, with salads and pastas. Prices are reasonable for the area. They keep cards and a range of board games to amuse those students who seek distraction from the daily grind. Outside in the massive beer garden there is seating for a couple of hundred people, and in the summer and during the Edinburgh Festival it is very busy indeed. Naturally, it attracts a lot of students being a stone's throw from George Square. Decorated in a traditional style, the Pear Tree was famous as a literary centre, being the home of the poet, Thomas Blacklock, back in the 18th Century. It was used as a whisky store for much of the 20th Century till being converted to a pub in 1982. Rumours abound that black-market whisky was available from 'broken' barrels but I only ever bought the one bottle. The building also houses a couple of other bars and a bistro. In the summer, the garden is used for live music on Sunday afternoons from 1-4pm, tending towards acoustic sounds. It is also regularly used as a Fringe venue. The Pear Tree's beer garden has proved popular with families with young children. The social mix on a hot summer's day (they do happen occasionally) is truly cosmopolitan. The toilets are adequate but up steep stairs.

The Southsider West Richmond Street *Managed*   E14

M-Th 11.30am-12am, F 11.30am-1am, S 11am-12am, Sun 12.30pm-12am
The Southsider is a pub managed on behalf of Maclay's, one of Scotland's smaller brewers, who make extremely fine cask

conditioned ale; they also stock a couple of guest ales at any one time. A range of over 20 malts and a good variety of real beer in bottles are also stocked. This is a pub that is soon to be refurbished. It has always had the feel of somebody's front room and it is comfortable. Both current rooms are about to be made into one open plan bar and it is hoped the welcoming atmosphere will not be too severely affected. The decor has never been startling – the beer is the attraction. They have a steady supply of regular customers from further afield than the local clientele who drink here, as well as a few students and lecturers dropping in. It seems particularly popular with mature students. It is also a place where various groups meet in the back room – and thus have an excuse to partake of the fine ales on offer. With jazz on once a month, the Southsider has carved a little niche market for itself amongst discerning drinkers who generally like a bit of peace and quiet – they do however put on quizzes on Sundays. I even know a Geordie in the Midlands who talks fondly of it – often. Prices are very resonable for the area, and the food, available from 12pm-2pm, is cooked on the premises and will not require a mortgage. Plain wholesome grub said the Man from Fife. He should know judging by his girth. Toilets fine and accessible.

The Moo Bar Buccleuch Street *Tenancy*   E15

M-Th 11am-1am, FS 12pm-1am, Sun 12.30pm-1am
Some bars should be entered sober. Why? Because if you go into them a little confused or overly elated you could be in for a shock. The Moo Bar is one of these. For many years known as the Meadow, this is a place that has had a history. It was the scene of all sorts of blues and bevvy madness in the 1960s; it then quietened down into a local community pub, and has now resurfaced in glorious eccentricity as the Moo Bar. Catering quite plainly for a young student type crowd they have keg beers, premiums lagers, lots of trendy bottled beers and alcopops – and also the dreaded absinthe. Maybe this was what the designer was on when the place was designed! With furniture from Job Lot the decor is based around sculptural variations on animals, specifically African cows – seriously. It has to be seen to be appreciated. The tin-can snake light over the bar is superb as is the wonderful white cow's head over the stairs leading to the upstairs bar. The upper level is done in French/Spanish Stone Age cave art style, with animals and hunting scenes. They have a limited lunchtime menu which always includes a veggie dish and in general the prices are on the high side. But what price inspired madness? At nights this quiet bar rocks to the sounds of DJs turning out reggae and hip-hop in the candlelit atmosphere. In the

day it is quiet with ambient music and a sporadic crowd of students and some locals, interspersed with the odd working stiff from nearby offices. If you are going to be different this is certainly one way to go about it. Amenities are fine but not very accessible.

McEwan's Ale House Clerk St *Managed*   E17

M-Th 11am-12am, FS 11am-1am, Sun 12.30pm-11pm
This is a decent-sized brewery managed pub which has a traditional Victorian aspect, with quite a bit of original memorabilia, mirrors and prints. These days it has a couple of real ales and standard range of spirits. Food, which is standard pub grub, includes soup and some dishes made on the premises. There is no entertainment other than the television and machines. The pub is pretty much a community based boozer, with cinema-goers from the Odeon opposite, occasional students and some passing tourists dropping in. This bar is named after William McEwan, local publican, brewer, Member of Parliament and Privy Councillor who was around a century or so ago. He was the founder of the giant brewery combine that now owns this pub. Thankfully they don't seem to meddle too much with this establishment. Reasonably priced. Toilets are down a set of pretty steep stairs.

The Cauldron Clerk Street *Chain*   E18

M-S12pm-1am, Sun12.30pm-1am
Pubs are important for more reasons than that they just sell drink. Conviviality, the chance to meet like minded people and to socialise in a relaxed atmosphere are all-important too. This accounts for the popularity of the Cauldron, which, though it has a couple of real ales and a fair range of whiskies and other spirits, is a wee bit on the scruffy side. Almost all the wall space is covered with posters advertising various so-called cultural activities. With long bench seating in nooks off the bar, it is in fact a little bit wild and woolly with its dark and moody decor. The regulars would probably see themselves as a kind of bohemian intelligentsia, and who am I to argue with that? One of the attractions is a truly eclectic juke box which combines all sorts of music from Billie Holliday to the Sisters of Mercy. This is a bar where whatever your thing is, it's OK with everyone else, and there is never any hassle. Therefore you will find bikers, goths, punks and the utterly indescribable. Primarily a late night hangout, no one is phased by transvestite bar persons or much else, though the Man from Fife said he thought it would be too much for his granny. If you can't find another pub you like, it

seems possible that this is the place for you. It therefore deserves a high rating for originality and tolerance, though they serve no food and the Halloween decorations stay up till being replaced by Christmas ones. It has some of the atmosphere of a basement Amsterdam café. Toilets tolerable and accessible.

Droothy Neebors Causewayside *Managed*   E20

M-S 11am-1am, Sun 12pm-1am
This is almost a Scottish theme pub – the name is Scots (still spoken by more than a third of the Scottish population) for thirsty neighbours though the suggestion is of a deep thirst and close neighbours – it is a very emotive language. With five cask ales, a couple of stouts, 25+ malt whiskies and its own label wine, there is a lot of choice in the fermented beverage area. Catering to the known restraint of students, they also offer jugs of beer and pitchers of cocktails at reduced prices. The bar is on two levels and very much traditionally derived, with bits of wooden barrels, old musical instruments and other cod authentic bric-a-brac subtly placed around the walls! The Scottishness of the place is underlined by the variety of prints and Burns' poems on the walls. They even go so far as to have live Scottish traditional music on occasion. As opposed to the dead sort you can still hear from time to time, said the Man from Fife, who is an aficionado of fiddle and accordion music – than which you can get no more traditional. Long Live Jimmy Shand! The clientele is local during the day but at nights and weekends it is pretty much a student haunt. They hold quizzes and sponsor three different student sports teams – guaranteeing a bit of custom, you would think. All in all, not a bad howff, but did Belhaven brewery have the same B&Q DIY kit as was apparently available for Irish theme pubs a year or two ago? Toilets fine but access difficult. The bar ghost here is said to knock the tops off whisky bottles on the gantry – oh yeah?

The Southern Bar South Clerk Street *Managed*   E21

M-W 12pm-12am, Th-S 12pm-1am, Sun 12pm-11am
This is a big brewery managed pub, which like a few others of its kind seems to have been allowed to flourish in its own identity. The layout has a couple of raised separate areas with a separate games machine area (including table football), and the decor can only be described as anarchic. It has clearly developed over time and retains some original Victorian features, such as the roof and some leaded glass. Some of the modern features are plain daftness; one section of wall near the door has a suggestion for complaints from a previous member of staff that is unusual and

rather pointed! The drinks are standard keg beers and lagers with an everyday range of spirits. Food is limited to hot snacks. Very much a student pub, the Southern sponsors a range of student sports teams and other academic/student societies. Its location near the Dick Veterinary College attracts a lot of custom. The management do various deals for students including a discount on one original feature; in-house Internet access, at reasonable rates. No doubt this will prove to be the start of a trend – for pubs wanting a younger clientele anyway. Apart from students, the pub attract bikers and the odd tourist heading in to the city. They have occasional live music and regular quizzes. Theme nights at the weekend feature such delights as fancy dress karaoke events. These prove popular amongst the locals – there is no accounting for tastes. It is obvious that the clientele, which peaks at the weekends, is drawn by the atmosphere generated in this interesting hotchpotch of a pub. Reasonably priced, the Southern has decent disabled amenities.

The Wine Glass Newington Road *Managed*   E22

M 12pm-11pm, T-Th 12pm-12am, FS 11.30am-1am, Sun 12.30pm-11pm

Located on the very edge of the guest house ghetto of Newington, the Wine Glass is a Brewery managed pub that attracts a lot of passing trade from visitors heading in towards the delights of the city centre. With no real ales but a wide range of keg beers, this smallish, rather spartan bar is very cheap 'n' cheerful. Food, which is not cooked on the premises, is the cheapest in the area and pretty much standard fare. With a small regular trade and some student trade, the Wine Glass makes its way off the tourist dollar in the summer, but like many other hostelries these days attracts custom for sporting events on the big screen. The impression one gets is that from the brewery's point of view it makes money, so why bother. Amenities OK.

The Junction Bar West Preston St *Managed*   E23

M-S 10.30am-1am, Sun 12.30pm-1am

The thing about brewery owned pubs is that though some are dire, others can spring a real surprise. The Junction is one of the latter. The decor is warm, modern, bright and almost Mediterranean, with tables and chairs and a few booths – be careful in the ones in the back room – only giants' feet can touch the floor sitting in these. A reasonably sized pub split into two main areas, a lot of thought has gone in to developing the Junction. With no real ales and standard keg beers and lagers, the Junction comes into its own with a good, if limited, wine list, a range of different boozy coffees and cocktails – with subtle names like Quickie, Slippery Nipple, Bloo and Bubblegum. They also provide that most modern of drinks – smoothies. These involve an arcane combination of fruit juices, yoghurt and alcohol and are said to prove popular. Your correspondent must admit to finding the idea confusing – is it a food or a drink? Drinks are reasonably priced for the area. The food, all cooked on the premises, veers towards the Spanish, is available till the early evening and is fairly priced and of good quality. The clientele is a varied one, including lunchtime suits, students and a strong regular local support. Many pubs these days have a big screen but here they use it imaginatively. Regulars come in to watch their favourite programmes as if it was a cinema, though as yet there are no plans for selling popcorn. As the programmes involved include Buffy the Vampire Slayer, Ally McBeal and the Simpsons, the clientele are obviously on the youngish side – though it should be remembered that Homer is a hero to slobs of all ages. Go Homey! Decent amenities.

Minders Causewayside *Free House*   E24

M-W 11am-12am, Th 11am-12.30am, FS 11am-1.30am, Sun 12.30pm-11am
This fine little free house on Edinburgh's South Side has a unique feel to it. A tasteful, almost art-deco like pub, it has a couple of real ales and a standard range of spirits. Primarily a local bar with a regular clientele, Minder's has a Happy Hour, with a substantial discount on its already reasonable prices from 5pm-8pm daily. With its subtle lighting, good quality prints on the wall and a range of bric-a-brac, the place has the feel of the reception area of a high-class high hotel! The decor reflects the owner's taste and is not designed to appeal to the youth market. Occasionally tourists drop in to sample the pleasant quietness of Minders. It is very well kept and the atmosphere is warm and friendly. The Man from Fife said he felt like he was at his auntie's house. Amenities are fine.

Leslie's Bar Ratcliffe Terrace *Free House*   E27

M-W 11am-11pm, Th 11am-11.30pm, F-S 11am-12.30am, Sun 12.30pm-11.30pm
There has been a tendency over the past few years for breweries and other chains to refurbish pubs in what they think is traditional Victorian style. Leslie's is the real thing. An architecturally superb bar with original fittings and decorations, this medium sized pub is a delight to the eye. Opened in 1896 it has always been privately owned and with the gorgeous gantry

behind the long bar, the superb cornices, outstanding decorative
plaster work and glorious leaded glass, you can not get a better
example of a late Victorian bar. The scale might not match that of
some of the city centre Victorian pubs, with their vast tiled areas,
but as a small to medium sized local hostelry it really is a
classic. With the magnificence of the surroundings, always
spotlessly clean, goes a dedication to customer service. There
are half a dozen well-kept real ales, a wine list of a dozen wines
and a good range of malt whiskies. Food is limited to pies and
snacks, as putting in a kitchen would change the pub – and that
is not to be contemplated! Long known for the quality of its beer
as much as its physical magnificence, Leslie's has a steady
regular clientele that see it as their community pub. Sons and
daughters follow their fathers and mothers as Leslie's regulars,
giving a relaxed and friendly atmosphere that welcomes the
tourist, many of whom come from the nearby guest-houses. This
is the kind of pub where the clientele range from 18 to 80 years
old and all are equally welcome. On Tuesday nights there is a
four piece jazz band playing a variety of styles. The Man from Fife
asked if they could move to Kirkcaldy!

Bar Kohl George IV Bridge *Free House*   E1

12pm-1am, closed Sunday (except Festival)
A very trendy place that is so cool it seems frigid. Very modern,
too American and not really friendly at all.

Negociants Lothian Street *Managed*   E7

9am-3am all week
The first of the café-bar type pubs to spring up looking for the
student market, maintains a good standard.

Abbey Buffet Clerk Street *Managed*   E19

M-S 11am-1am, Sun 12.30pm-12am
Traditional style brewery run pub that we did not find particularly
hospitable.

Bierex Causewayside *Free House*   E25

10am-1am all week
Opening as we go to print this modern, trendy, bright pub takes
over from an old favourite, Jamie's.

The Old Bell Causewayside *Chain*   E29

M-Th 11am-11.45pm, FS 11am-12.45am, Sun 11am-11.45pm
Fascinating old pub, full of bells, which was refurbished at the
start of the new millennium. Hope it is as good.

The Doctors Forrest Road *Managed*   E6

M-Th 11am-12am, FS 11am-1am, Sun 12.30pm-11pm
A fair attempt at an old fashioned feeling for this big roomy pub.
Tends to be popular with students which doesn't have to be a
bad thing!

Rutherford's Drummond *Free House*   E10

M-S 11am-11pm, Sun 6.30pm-11pm
Well worth a visit for the interesting Robert Louis Stevenson
memorabilia. He used to take a drink here himself before heading
for sunnier climes.

Stewart's Bar Drummond Street *Managed*   E11

M-S 11am-12am, Sun 11am-11pm
Once a fine example of a local community pub with a great
atmosphere, now sadly a shadow of its former self. Notable lamp
post outside the front door.

Proctor's Buccleuch Street *Free House*   E16

11am-12.30am all week
A fine and cosy little bar, clean and well-kept. Despite being close
to the University few students drink here, though the odd lecturer
can be seen occasionally (a lot of them are).

ROSE STREET

This street, which runs parallel to Princes Street to the north, is famous for pub crawls. Generations of adolescent Scots males have tried to drink their way along Rose Street by having a drink in every one of its bars. At various times, these have numbered up to 17 or so, particularly if, as we have done here, you include the Café Royal and Guildford Arms at the east end of Princes Street. You could, of course, be even more insane and include the two or three others within a few yards of the central route. Be that as it may – and imagine trying this when the streets are awash with drunken rugby supporters all trying to do the same thing – these days Rose Street is a touch more sophisticated. In fact, whatever your taste in drinking you should be able to find something here you like. It is a part of town that most weekends is not particularly genteel, but still the odd quiet nook can be found for a bit of sophisticated drinking. A few years ago the street was pedestrianised and since then the shopping has improved considerably. It is in fact a fine place for a Saturday afternoon, drifting from shop to shop and pub to pub as the mood takes you. In this section we have a few of Edinburgh's finest, like the Café Royal, The Kenilworth and the Guildford Arms; pubs that would stand out *in any city, but some of the smaller bars like No 37 and the Gordon Arms are well worth a visit too. The range of pub grub, too, is considerable from the traditional splendour of the Abbotsford and the upmarket fare of Dirty Dick's to the more mundane but acceptable eats in the Hogshead or Breck's. Time always brings change. Though much has improved, Milne's Bar is no longer what it was and the recent closure of the brewing side of the now ineptly named Rose Street Brewery are not steps in the right direction. However, this probably remains the most famous drinking street in Scotland, if not the UK.*

Guildford Arms West Register Street *Managed*   **F1**

M-Thu 11am-11pm, FS 11am-12am, Sun 11am-11pm
This magnificent Victorian Boozer lies just off the east end of Princes Street on the north side beside Register House. Originally built as a store in 1841 it was eventually converted to its current magnificence in the 1890s. The ornate cornices on the soaring ceiling, the magnificent canopy, the windows and the gantry are all first class. Through the back by the food counter there is a sunken table, which can lead to the odd problem after sampling some of the pub's sterling range of real beers. This is very much a city centre pub and is rarely quiet. It is a meeting place for locals on a night out at the weekends, for all sorts of clubs and groups and for visitors to the city; for concerts, rugby matches and that little known annual event, the Edinburgh Festival – usually the cue for locals to disappear and rent out their flats! For many years now, the Guildford has been supplying an ever changing and thoughtful range of delights for the real beer drinking fraternity and some of them have to be treated with respect. Or perhaps that's not what you want to do. The food is good pub grub and reasonably priced; despite its city centre location, the drink prices are acceptable too. Beware though – many an unwary crew has gathered to start off in the Guildford and head elsewhere only to find the last bell ringing. The staff are pleasant and the pub always well-kept. If you like busy, noisy pubs – with no canned music – or are a fan of the mind shifting effects of cask conditioned ale, you can hardly do better. The revolving door can cause the odd problem for visitors with luggage or musicians with cases – more often on the way out than the way in!

Café Royal Register Place *Managed*   F2

M-W 11am-11pm, Th 11am-12pm, FS 11am-1am, Sun 12.30pm-
1am
In the same block as the Guildford Arms, the Café is in the same
class. With five cask ales, 17 malts, three Irish and a limited
wine list, it offers less for the real beer fiend but does a classier
line in food. This is all from the restaurant next door and is
probably the most expensive pub food in town. However, if you
want lobster bisque and fresh oysters you do have to pay. Food
prices, for the quality, are very good. Beer prices are city centre
standard. The real glory of this place is the decor – all of which is
protected by law. The magnificent oval bar with stand-up lighting,
the glorious frosted glass windows and the carved wood and
mirrored wall between bar and restaurant all are first class. On
the south wall are a series of painted tile panels that are truly
wonderful, depicting a series of inventors including Caxton,
Faraday, Newton, Stevenson and Watt; without whom the modern
world would not be as it is. These are a glorious late Victorian
tribute to the idea of Progress, and are stunning. The roof and
cornices are absolute classics of the late Victorian period and the
banquette seating around the windows speak of elegance. Always
a place to see and be seen, the Café is very Edinburgh. The
clientele is mixed with a lot of professional people, rugby players
and fans, students and of course tourists. The Man from Fife
thought it a bit OTT, but admired the decor. Down the years
staffing has always been a problem here, affecting the service,
but the manger reckons he now has 'a wonderful little team to
suit your every need'. We shall see. The wonderful Victorian
toilets are down steep stairs.

Tiles St Andrew's Square *Chain*   F3

M-Th 11am-11pm, FS 11am-12am Sun 12.30pm-11am – but not
in the Winter.
Three real ales served, a couple of dozen malts and a good wine
list at fair prices for the area. Food is cooked in house and is
high-class pub grub, served 11am-5pm Monday to Friday and
11am-7pm on a Saturday. An à la carte menu is soon to be
added. This is yet another one time bank and the origin of its
name is obvious – even from outside. Another riot of Victorian
tiling, Tiles has an oblong central bar amid the floral tiles and
mirrors covering the walls and pillars, and beneath superb
cornices and magnificent vaulting arches. There is plenty of
seating, and in the summer they have tables and chairs out on
the pavement – trés continental! Much of their custom consists

of regulars, though they do attract lots of office workers, shoppers and tourists during the day. Amenities fine, but access difficult.

The Abbotsford Rose Street *Free House*   F4

M-S 11am-11pm, Sun closed
This is a superb bar which stocks up to eight real ales at any one time with over 70 malts and a limited list of wines. For many years the Abbotsford has been well known for the quality both of it's drink and it's food. One of the first pubs in town to serve food, the menu veers toward the traditional and is the same in the bar as it is in the restaurant. Lunch is available in the bar and the restaurant from 12pm till 3pm and from 5.30pm till 10pm upstairs. The tradition of lunch at the Abbotsford is one that several generations of city natives have grown up with. The fittings throughout are original from when it opened in 1901 and the heavily pillared central bar is a magnificent example of late Victoriana. A dark almost sombre-looking pub, with magnificent cornices and superb panelling, the Abbotsford is quietly elegant. Two walls have long bench seating below the plain mirrors and at lunchtimes the place is a hive of activity with local business people, shoppers, tourists and the odd journalist – most of them are quite odd, actually. The bar has been owned by the same family since 1940 and the third generation carries on the tradition well. Mrs Grant who had the bar in the 1940s and 50s was one of a trio of fearsome Edinburgh publicans who included Mrs Scott, whose pub was at the other end of the street, and Betty Moss, who had the original Old Chain Pier down by the river. The attraction of the Abbotsford is such that one of the two dozen or so Saturday lunch regulars has been coming in weekly for 52 years! At the weekends the crowd is a bit younger. Service is always fast and efficient. The toilets are classically Victorian; wheelchair access is a little problematic.

Milne's Bar Rose Street/Hanover Street *Managed*   F6

M-Th 11am-12am, FS 11am-1am, Sun 12.30pm-11.30pm
This is a curious hotch-potch of a place that has recently been substantially enlarged and is now on two floors. They have up to ten cask ales, a dozen or so malts and carry a range of heritage beers and a wine list of nine wines. One downstairs room is a dining room with table service but you can eat anywhere. The menu is standard and available at lunch and evening. The new bar on Rose Street is cod-traditional with wood panelling and the usual type of prints. Downstairs is the original Milne's, the home of Edinburgh's poets in the old days. It seems anomalous to

make a feature of dead poets and then fill it with blaring pop music! The Man from Fife remembers it as once it was and couldn't get out fast enough. This is the original bar that gave rise to the name the Poets' Pub. For much of the middle years of the 20th Century this was the meeting place for a host of Scotland's leading literary figures. Hugh MacDiarmid could be seen drinking with Sydney Goodsir Smith, with Edwin Morgan reading a book and Hamish Henderson discussing the relevance of oral literature at the bar with Norman McCaig. The influence of twentieth century Scottish poetry in particular was greatly enhanced by the gatherings in Milne's, as was the ongoing revival of the Scots language in modern contemporary literature – a revival that continues with at least one science-fiction novel in Scots now on the horizon. Much has been made of recent political developments in Scotland but the cultural Renaissance that has been taking place these last few decades was always fuelled by conviviality and whisky – and no more so than here in Milne's Bar. For those with a specific interest there is a magnificent painting of Milne's in its heyday in the Scottish National Portrait Gallery round in Queen Street. Disabled toilets upstairs.

No. 37 Rose Street *Free House*   F8

M-S 11am-11pm, Sun 12.30pm-7pm
Robertson's Number 37 as it is known is a distinctive little pub that looks quiet, even sedate from outside – but a lot goes on in here. Though they have 2 cask ales in good condition the real feature of Robertson's is malt whisky. They stock well over a hundred malts and a further 16 Irish whiskies. This brings visitors from all over the world and several of Edinburgh's fine whisky shops send potential customers here to sample before they buy. The bar features in several books on whisky but still has its own regular clientele. The L-shaped bar is comfortable and retains some original 1901 features including the magnificent gantry. Outside, the Robertson's coat of arms says it all – malt specialists. The same family has owned it since opening; it can be fairly said that they've a world-wide reputation and many tourists find their way in. Food is restricted to snacks, sandwiches and pies. This is a stop on many of the city's guided tours and regularly has television soap stars reading over their lines in the seating area round the back. There is no juke box or fruit machine and they feel no need to stage entertainment here. The clientele tends towards the middle-aged and includes lawyers and business people and retired people from all walks of life. All in all this is a terrific little pub that so enthused the Man from Fife that he was trying to figure out how many nights it would

take him to sample the entire stock! Such things have been tried before and are not to be recommended, though during the recent Rugby World Cup the Spanish team had a good go at it! Reasonably priced and with excellent service, No. 37 is worth a visit. Toilets are down steep stairs.

Fling and Firkin Rose Street *Chain* F9

11am-1am, Sun 12.30pm-1am
Yet another variation on the theme of mock traditional chain pubs (at least in its name this is an odd wee bar). Once famous as Paddy's Bar, it is a bit nondescript nowadays. The decor is bright, as are the staff, and supposedly quaint mottoes abound on the walls. They have only keg beers but a good range of wines to accompany the internationally inclined pub grub served from 12.30pm-8pm. Only the specials are actually cooked on the premises. Prices are pretty good for Rose Street. This is a pub which attracts a lot of passing trade from shoppers, local workers and a smattering of regulars. At the weekends it changes significantly and attracts a lot of pre-clubbers in from the suburbs with DJs on Friday and Saturday nights. Amenities are fine and accessible.

Rose Street Brewery Rose Street *Managed* F10

M-Th 11am-11pm, FS 11am-12am, Sun 12.30pm-8pm
Opened as part of the fashion for brewing local ales that derived from the real ale phenomenon, this biggish pub shows what is wrong with big brewery and other chains. Recently taken over in the giant Monopoly style take-overs plaguing the pub industry, the first thing the new owners did was sack the Brewer. Thus at a stroke they destroyed what made this an interesting and different pub, while at the same time depriving the country of the notoriously strong Auld Reekie Ale which was brewed here. Decisions taken miles away from the customer base are generally crass and this is no exception. Now the Brewery has only two cask ales They continue to serve food from 11.30am-9.30pm and the imitation traditional pub still brings in tourists and the passing trade. Friendly bar staff and amenities upstairs.

Victoria and Albert Frederick Street *Chain* F11

M-S 12pm-12am, Sun 12.30pm-10pm
This is clearly modelled on a traditional English pub and has extensive restaurant accommodation aimed at the tourist market. With a limited range of keg beers and only six malts, but an extensive wine list, this is not the place you would expect

regulars. You would be wrong. There is in fact a tight group of
regular customers. The extensive à la carte menu of the
restaurant is available in the bar 12pm-3pm. The bar itself is
quite plush, with its low ceiling making the place quite cosy. The
piano is available for any customer who feels like rattling the
ivories – sixteen verses of some obscure Chinese folk-song from
the Man from Fife soon showed the folly of that. Saturday night
the musical fare improves with swing-oriented jazz. They also
have an open mike for would-be stand up comedians on Sundays.
Amenities fine but up stairs.

Breck's Rose Street *Managed*   F12

M-S 10.30am-1am, Sun 12.30pm-11pm
This big square pub with another room to the back has a fine
central bar. They have one cask ale, a selection of keg beers, a
dozen malts and half a dozen wines. Food is heated on the
premises and served from 12pm-7pm. Unlike many Edinburgh
pubs they don't serve haggis, but will provide Cajun snacks and
Italian dishes. The pub is supposedly based around the fictional
Highlander Alan Breck, who figures strongly in Robert Louis
Stevenson's *Kidnapped*, but there are only a few references. This
is a pub that attracts tourists and a lot of passing trade. Like
most city centre pubs, it has a lot of party types and pre-clubbers
at the weekend and on Friday and Saturday they have DJs. The
back room is comfortable and even has a few shelves of books
for quiet contemplation. Amenities fine but downstairs.

The Gordon Arms Rose Street *Managed*   F13

M-Th 10am-11pm, FS 10am-12pm, Sun 12.30pm-8.30pm
The Gordon Arms sells keg beers, lager and the usual suspects
at the lowest prices for miles around! Giving the larger measure
of 35mls for spirits, they are still cheaper than all their
competition. Food consists of filled rolls and sandwiches. This is
a pretty plain pub with a small bar, a fair amount of seating,
wood panelling and a plain wooden floor. There are interesting old
prints on the walls. Although they get some of the weekend party
crowd in, the Gordon has a steady clientele of regulars from all
over the town, some passing trade, shoppers and suits at 5
o'clock, but very few tourists. This is a shame because this, we
were assured, is an actual 'real Scottish pub.' As the manager
put it, 'the formula is simple; cheap drink, happy atmosphere and
good craic – and no idiots allowed.' Amenities fine but no
disabled access.

The Kenilworth Rose Street *Managed*   F14

M-Th 9am-11pm, FS 9am-12.45am, Sun 12.30pm-11pm,
Another of Edinburgh's fine historic pubs, the Kenilworth is a
visual delight from the lovely wood and glass frontage through to
the quiet family room at the back. The entire building is listed
and is full of beautiful tiling, glorious original mirrors and
excellent leaded glass. It has a striking big mahogany bar with
original gas light fittings converted to electricity. The gantry, too,
is original as are the chandeliers and clock – all dating from the
conversion of an original home into a pub in 1904. The building
itself dates from 1789. The whole place was tastefully and
sympathetically restored in the late 1980s. Apart from the
architectural delights, this is a well run pub that does a very good
trade in food. With the kitchen on the premises there is a range
of fairly priced high quality pub grub available from noon till nine
o'clock. They stock six real ales, over 50 malt whiskies and a
reasonable wine list. The room at the back (look out for the
stained glass Tam O' Shanter) is a designated family room and
proves very popular with local families with young children – my
son remembers it well – even to the extent of having high chairs
for the little ones. This is a bar that fully deserves its place in the
Historic Pubs Guide. The clientele in the Kenilworth is very mixed
with families with kids, business suits, shoppers and a lot of
tourists all coming through its doors. Being in Rose Street it can
get hectic at the weekends, when like most of the bars in the
area it attracts the younger crowd. Whether you have a young
family or not the Kenilworth is always worth a visit. Amenities
fine – wheelchair access round the back.

Scott's Rose Street *Chain*   F19

M-Th 11am-11pm, TF-S 11am-1am, Sun 6.30pm-11pm
Now part of a large chain of pubs, Scott's was well known for
many years because of its redoubtable landlady, known far and
wide as Ma Scott. Not a lady for taking any prisoners, the Man
from Fife was expelled many years ago for having the audacity to
complain about the slowness of the service. Not only was he
summarily barred, but so were the rest of us who were with him!
During this stramash Ma Scott moved not an inch from her
customary seat beside the till – she was the only one ever to
operate that particular piece of equipment! She was a favourite
amongst rugby fans who only visited the Capital for international
matches, and many were the tales told about her. Though long
gone to that great bar-room in the sky, an aged American
gentlemen dropped in during the 1998 Edinburgh Festival and

enquired after Mrs Scott, whom he had met many years ago. As
ever, she had clearly made an impression. These days, Scott's
stocks four real ales, a standard half a dozen malts and a wine
list of nine wines with all the usual bottles, but no cocktails.
Food, available till 7pm, is pub-grub, including such exotic items
as burritos alongside haggis and burgers. All are cooked on the
premises but, we were told, there are no chips! The low-roofed
room with its U-shaped bar retains some original fittings, and is
pretty traditional looking with a lot of posters on the walls. Like
most Rose Street pubs, it has passing trade during the week,
with both local and out-of-town regulars and the mad mob at the
weekend. Still gets lots of rugby fans on match days. Amenities
fine but no disabled access to the gents.

The Hogshead Rose Street/Castle Street *Managed*   F15

M-S 11am-1am, Sun 12.30pm-1am
With seven cask ales, 13 malts, and a wine list of 15, this is a
large, bright and light coloured basement bar. Much like an
English alehouse with its exposed brickwork and wood panelling,
they provide an extensive and varied menu, but only the daily
specials are cooked in-house. Food is available 11am-9pm during
the week, but till 8pm on Fridays and Saturdays when the place
tends to fill up with lots of hen and stag parties. It's very much a
case of 'lights down and music up' in the Hogshead. One special
offer is that you can buy a 'bat' of beer, which is four different
cask ales, each in a third of a pint, allowing the sampling of all
four without losing one's equilibrium. Prices are very fair for the
city centre. Amenities acceptable, though obviously downstairs.

Filthy McNasty's Rose Street *Chain*   F16

M-Th 11am-11pm, FS 11am-1am, Sun 12.30pm-11pm
The joke of the name is the most striking thing about this Rose
Street boozer. A smallish, square bar, they serve only keg beers
and lagers, though they stock a dozen malt whiskies. Food is
standard, available at lunchtimes, but not cooked on the
premises. With a few bits of tartan, some interesting old
domestic artefacts and a few Scottish posters about the place,
there is an attempt at a theme but it is pretty plain and
unassuming. The lovely big window gives a good view of the
street and is a grand spot for people watching over a pint. At
weekends, they put on DJs to pull in the younger crowd, and they
get a lot of hen and stag parties. During the week it is mainly
shoppers and tourists they attract. Amenities accessible and
adequate.

The Rose and Crown Rose Street *Tenancy*   F17

12pm-1am all week, except Sundays, opening at 12.30pm
Though they stock only keg beers and half a dozen malts, the
Rose has a good range of bottled spirits and beers and a list of
shooters and pitchers. Food is bar snacks available till 10pm. A
boozer of long standing reputation, it is a bit nondescript now,
though brightly painted and clean with a few posters on the walls;
it has a cosy air about it. Their main trade in the week is
shoppers and suits at lunchtime and 5 o'clock, and we were told
it gets a bit like a staff room for local office workers. Monday
nights, they have acoustic music and at the weekends they are
part of the Rose Street mayhem when the party people hit the
town, though they do have a core of regular customers. Amenities
are adequate but upstairs.

Dirty Dick's Rose Street *Free House*   F18

M-Th 11am-11pm, FS 11am-1am, Sun 12.30pm-11pm
This is a contradictory place indeed. Named after a supposedly
historical character in the days before plumbing whose job it was
to remove night soil from houses, Dirty Dick's is in fact a pretty
upmarket place. There has been a pub here since 1859, though
today it is almost like a bistro. With at least half a dozen real
beers at any one time, a dozen or so malt whiskies and a decent
wine list, they put a lot of effort into the food. Cooked in-house
with a high class menu, they serve food till 10pm during the
week, 7pm at weekends. Given the quality, it is not surprising
that for both food and drink this place is on the expensive side.
The decor is a clutter of bric-a-brac on the walls, with old toys,
military uniforms and musical instruments; with the low ceiling
and subdued lighting, it has a comfortable, almost homely
atmosphere. Another place where candles are a fixture, there is
what can only be called a candle sculpture opposite the bar which
is unique. During the week they do a good trade with business
types and tourists. At the weekends they have a more sedate
atmosphere than many of the other pubs nearby, with a lot of
people booking in for early dinner then staying on to have a few
drinks – very civilised. The staff wear waistcoats, and though
upmarket it is not obnoxiously so. Even the Fifer had to admit
that, grudgingly. They have a couple of outside tables, making it a
grand place in the summer to sit and watch the world go by.
Definitely a place with a character all its own. Amenities fine and
accessible.

The Auld Hundred Rose Street *Managed*   F5

M-Th 11am-11pm, FS 11am-12am, Sun 12.30pm-5pm
Fine old Rose Street bar with some notable bar fittings, like the
gold painted cast iron rails and some leaded glass. It now
includes a bistro upstairs – trés traditional.

The Three Tuns Hanover Street *Managed*   F7

M 12pm-7pm, T 12pm-10pm, WTh 12pm-11pm, FS 12pm-1am,
Sun closed
Somewhat drab basement bar with all day food (and loud music)
calling itself Edinburgh's best kept secret – modesty is always
the best policy.

NEW TOWN

For logistical reasons these pubs have been grouped under the heading of the New Town, while some of them, especially in George Street, are closer to Rose Street. However Rose Street is a definable area in its own right. Edinburgh's New Town is described extensively elsewhere, but it is a delight to discover on foot; and several of the hostelries herein mentioned are in their own way a delight too. With the general upgrading of pubs over the last few years, placing a much heavier emphasis on service and quality, the once famous Edinburgh reserve (in the other place they say there's more fun at a Glasgow stabbing than at an Edinburgh wedding) is no longer in evidence. This might be due to the fact that many of the staff in bars are young, well-educated and professional – though the idea that youth and good looks are more important than efficiency and courtesy, allied to experience, is one which seems to dominate in some quarters.

Bar 38 George Street *Managed*   G5

M-S 10am-1am, Sun 10am-12am
It has been said that this showpiece bar is the future; the Man from Fife has said that if it is, he'll make sure he isn't around

much longer. A vast, bright converted office with an interesting
line in textile wall hangings (that might derive from Australian
Aboriginal art) Bar 38 is so cool it borders on the frigid. Draught
beers are all keg and include premium lagers, and they have a
wine list of a dozen and a very interesting range of vodkas. They
do a range of cocktails and carry lots of different bottled beers.
Food is available 10am-9.30pm and the menu is extensive,
trendy and caters for vegetarians. Prices for the food are a little
higher than the norm while the drinks are very pricey. The
weekday crowd of shoppers, office workers and tourists is
replaced at the weekends by the young pre-club set. The unisex
space between the gents and ladies is stunning with the
occasional young lass straying into the gents to admire the
equipment. Or not. Disabled access.

Madogs George Street *Free House*   G3

M-S 12pm-3am, Sun 6.30pm-3am
This is really a basement cocktail bar rather than a pub, but it is
a well-established Edinburgh institution. With cocktails, a wide
range of bottled beers, a dozen malts and a very wide range of
other spirits, this is a bar for the sophisticate; the Man from Fife
felt ill at ease till he realised the happy hour ran from 5pm-9pm.
Prices are generally mid range – for the area. The menu is more
that of a brasserie than a bar, with lots of seafood, but the prices
are reasonable indeed. Every night except Friday they have
music; Thursdays and Saturdays a band, the other nights a solo
pianist. The place gets busy late on most nights. During the day
and early evening they have the usual mix of clientele with
shoppers, some business people and tourists. Amenities fine.

All Bar One George Street *Chain*   G2

M-Th 11.30am-12am, FS 11.30am-1am, Sun 12.30pm-12am
Yet another converted bank, this large, bright and very simply
designed bar veers towards the wine bar rather than the
traditional Scottish pub. They have a couple of real beers,
premium lagers and a wine list of about 20. The target customer
base is clearly the over-21 (would-be) sophisticates of the city
and tends to range from about 25-40 years of age. There is a
considerable coterie of the fairer sex; that may sound like a
gratuitously sexist remark to make, but If you were standing
beside the Man from Fife you would realise the truth of it. The
menu is extensive, all cooked in-house and, like the drinks, not
particularly cheap. Trendy upmarket pub grub is available till
10pm. There is table service, and all of the long tables around
the main room have the interesting addition of handbag clips – a

feature designed to bolster the female friendly aspect of the bar.
The gantry is like a series of pigeonholes filled with wine bottles.
Although a large place, they keep the numbers down to about half
the legal maximum of 400 to ensure comfort for all; a policy
some other city centre pubs might like to learn from. This is done
by employing door-staff; the norm for late night city centre
hostelries these days.

The Standing Order George Street *Chain*   G1

M-S 11am-1am, Sun 12.30pm-1am
This massive converted bank (George Street is changing from a
banking district into a drinking centre) is a well thought out pub
that takes advantage of the original 19th Century decor. The
building features a magnificent vaulted ceiling, with some
interesting rooms off the main bar and a 27 ton safe still in situ!
With eight cask conditioned ales, a wide range of keg and bottled
beers, 21 malt whiskies and a wine list of a dozen, they do
provide a wide choice. The same can be said of the food, though
it is all brought in and only heated on the premises. The prices,
however, are very good with a lunchtime special of a burger and
chips and a pint of real beer available for £3.00 – excellent
value. There are all sorts of deals for meals and with up to 32
staff they do try and provide good service. This is bar that wants
everyone to feel at home, from the 'ties and mobile phone' crowd
to grannies out for lunch. There is absolutely no music, the
intention being to encourage conversation and a convivial
atmosphere – it seems to work though our Fife friend was a bit
overawed. They attract a steady passing trade and also a lot of
groups at the weekend. The bookcases on the wall opposite the
long bar are stocked with books from Oxfam and people do
actually read them – they can be taken home for a small
contribution to the sick kids' hospital. All in all, a slick, well
organised concept of a pub that deserves its level of success.
Especially as its staff reckon they are the best paid in the town.
Amenities are fine but down stairs.

The Drum and Monkey Queen Street *Managed* G6

M-Th 11.30am-11pm, FS 12pm-12am, Sun closed
This oddly named bar has three real ales, 15 malt whiskies and
an extensive wine list of 20 – four of them champagnes. With
prices a touch on the high side, it clearly sees itself as an
upmarket hostelry. Food, which is high-class pub fare, is not
cheap but all fresh and cooked on the premises. A broad range
includes New York Caesar salad and haggis. The kitchen is open
till 8pm. The Drum and Monkey name was the choice of the

original owner who had similar establishments in London and the Other Place (Edinburgh parlance for Glasgow). There is a startling structure of a Monkey on a Drum in a glass case, but the staff were unable to explain the mystery of the name. The Man from Fife said the place was over the top and had the air of a Barcelona bordello about it – I took this to mean it is plush and comfortable. Cosy it certainly is, with armchairs and a series of book lined booths in one of the back rooms for the more literate customer. With a steady daytime trade from office workers, shoppers and tourists, this big bar with interesting small rooms and quiet corners tends to be quieter at evenings and weekends, attracting discerning couples who like a bit of peace. They have a small clan of faithful regulars, many of whom are wine drinkers – but this is definitely a pub, not a wine bar. The management encourage anyone competent enough to have a go at the piano in the bar. With its imposing exterior, the Drum looks like it might be bit pretentious but is actually rather a fine boozer. Disabled toilets.

The Cambridge Bar Young Street *Chain*   **G7**

M-S 11am-1am, Sun closed
This is a pub that is very proud of its beers. With six cask ales always available, they were voted Edinburgh's CAMRA Pub of the Year for 1999. They also stock a dozen or so malt whiskies and the usual spirits, with an interesting range of heritage bottled beers. Food is available till 2.30pm and is cooked in house – the speciality being mussels in red wine. Prices for food are very good and for beer are reasonable. The bar is decorated in traditional style with lots of wood and bare brickwork, and has plush seating. Obviously attracting a lot of beer aficionados, they do steady office trade for lunch during the week and attract quite a few groups and societies. This medium sized two room bar is kept spotless, and the beer is always their prime consideration. Amenities fine – wheelchair access round the back.

The Oxford Bar Young Street *Tenancy*   **G8**

M-S 11am-1am, Sun 12.30pm-12am
With 3 real beers available and an excellent selection of malt whiskies, this pub is an Edinburgh institution; to such an extent, it even crops up in Ian Rankin novels. The tiny bar has not been remodelled in any way for many years. Food is restricted to pies and snacks. It is plain to the point of dowdiness, but this doesn't bother its customers in the least. For a long time run by a remarkable gentleman called Willie Ross, the Oxford passed into legend because of him. Refusing to stock more than the

minimum drink necessary for survival, with no such fripperies as
food available either, his cantankerousness was famous. If Willie
decided he didn't like you – how you looked, how you behaved or
how you spoke – he would throw you out without hesitation. Being
a particularly virulent type of Scottish nationalist, he would often
refuse to serve anyone he thought to be English – and some say
that this is why the Oxford became so well-frequented! The
regulars who drink here, and many come from distant parts of
the city, think of it more as a club than a pub and it certainly has
a warm and homely feel to it. Tourists who find their way here
often do so because of its entry in the Good Beer and CAMRA
Guides. During the week they have a steady office trade and this
is a stopping off point for a few organised tours. Several outdoor
sports groups gather in the interesting back room where the
management encourage live music sessions. The cleaners refuse
to go into the cellar which is thought to be haunted. Amenities
serviceable, but up a steep flight of half a dozen stairs.

Lord Bodo's Dublin Street *Free House*   **G12**

M-S 11am-1am, Sun 12.30pm-1am
One cask ale, keg beers, upwards of a dozen malts, eight wines
and a range of cocktails are available here. This small bright
basement bar has food from 12pm-6pm, including roast meats.
Steak and pasta are served at reasonable city centre prices. The
stone walls and wooden furniture with wrought iron and glass
features make this a trendy sort of place; but the low roof and
smallish size give it a comfortable feel. With a trade of local
office workers and shoppers during the day, they have a steady
regular evening trade, which includes tourists. Named after a
famous 18th Century judge, Lord Bodo's puts on a Monday night
quiz and are thinking of including live music on other nights.
Although not one of Edinburgh's classic pubs, this is a pleasant
little howff that is well-kept and well run. Amenities fine but no
disabled access.

The Star Bar Dublin Meuse *Tenancy*   **G14**

12pm-1am all week
This interesting two level bar tucked away in the New Town has a
couple of cask ales and a pretty standard range of other drinks.
The menu, which aims for that home-cooked style, features food
that is all cooked in the kitchen and available till 3pm. It includes
both the traditonal and trendy and is reasonably priced, as is the
drink. The decor is warm and comforting with no attempts at
mock traditional, and the bar itself is very small. This is offset by
plenty of seating on the upper level. The crowd is a mix of locals

and sporty types; the Star sponsors three teams playing rugby and hockey. The staff are very friendly and efficient. All in all a nice wee nook in the New Town, with just a hint of a social club atmosphere. Amenities fine but up stairs.

Clark's Bar Dundas Street *Chain*   G16

M-W 11am-11pm, Th-S 11am-11.30pm, Sun 12.30pm-11pm
Some pubs have reputations for a good pint of beer going back many years before the current taste for cask conditioned ales developed – Clark's is one of them. Today they stock five real ales and 50 or so malt whiskies, served in the larger measure of 35mls. This echoes the old tradition in Scottish pubs where the better ones tended to serve whisky and other lesser spirits in quarter gills, as opposed to the more normal fifth. Today the respective measures are 25 and 35mls. Food is restricted to filled rolls. Clarks is a plain squarish bar with two back rooms that have wall seating and tables, where in the bad old days females tended to be hidden away. Clark's is in no way ostentatious though it does have its visual delights. The pub was opened in 1899 and celebrated its centenary by having two murals of Dundas Street over the century painted on the walls of the steep stairs leading to the toilets. These are very witty, incorporating a lot of contemporary references from different periods and well worth a look. The clientele these days is mainly 'ties and phones' types from local offices during the day, but at all times it has a steady core of loyal regulars many of whom come from quite a long distance away and include tradesmen, university lecturers, shopkeepers and the odd scribe. Although they do show sport they make few other allowances for modern entertainment, and even the fruit machine is hidden downstairs between the toilets. This is a pub where the craic – the social intercourse between people happy in each others' company – is the main attraction, apart from the beer which is always in tip-top condition. We lost the Man from Fife after visiting Clark's and he wasn't found until two days later – in Glasgow.

Fibber Magee's Howe Street *Managed*   G18

M 11am-11pm, TW 11am-12am, Th-S 11am-1am, Sun 12.30pm-12am
As a brewery-run Irish theme pub, this should be a hard pub for your correspondent to like. However, although supposedly Irish themed, some of the wrought iron work, particularly on the lights over the bar, put me in mind of the Paris Metro! Trés art-deco! In fact, if you ignore the cod-Irishness, it's actually not bad but what these places actually have to do with Ireland is beyond my ken! With the big breweries more intent on listening to accountants than

to people who actually frequent their premises, such 'theming' will
no doubt continue. This is ironic given that what actually makes a
bar is its atmosphere, service and clientele; aspects of life that
have never been susceptible to number-crunching, a fact very well
understood in Ireland! In both the upstairs and downstairs bars
there are of course Irish street signs, bits of wooden bric-a-brac
and other cod-Irish tat but I am assured they are trying to wriggle
out from under this particular limitation. The basic design with
rough-cast walls and solid wood fittings is not unpleasant, and the
staff are friendly and efficient. The drinks on offer are pretty
standard, though having two stouts is no doubt a testament to its
Irishness. Food is again a bit cod-Irish and available till the evening.
Breakfast and brunch are featured. Although like most theme bars
subtlety is not on offer, the pub does attract a mixed clientele with
some office people and other suits through the day and a lot of
locals and mature students in the evenings. The lower bar doubles
as a function room. The management occasionally put on live
music, again tending towards 'Irishness'. The place serves as a
meeting place for some local community groups. Amenities
perfectly acceptable.

Kay's Jamaica Street West *Free House*   **G19**

M-Th 11am-12am, FS 11am-1am, Sun 12.30pm-11pm
This small bar, with a back room used for diners during the day,
does very good business. Originally the offices of Kay's wine
importers, it transmogrified into a pub a couple of decades ago.
Definitely a must for those with an interest in real beer, Kay's has
nine cask conditioned ales, at fair prices, and a range of some 70
malt whiskies. The interesting and traditional looking decor is
based on the old importing business with trade boards, barrels and
a host of interesting fittings matched with plush upholstery. The
coal fire is a particularly attractive feature and there is no canned
music – blessed relief! Regularly booked out for lunch, at that time
of the day the smell of traditional food being cooked upstairs gives
a warm, homely feel. The menu is available from 12pm-2.30pm
and the back room can be booked in advance. But this is no
restaurant or café bar! The clientele consists of a host of loyal
regulars coming from all over the city, drawn by the quality of the
beer and the fine service. They include professional people,
businessmen, lecturers and beer freaks from the mid-20s upwards.
On a Friday night the custom is usually about 90% regulars, so
there is no need for quizzes or other 'entertainment' here. This is a
bar whose sporting interests lean towards rugby rather than
football, and cribbage rather than dominoes. Kays is unashamedly
aimed at the top end of the market. The Man from Fife tried hard
to dislike Kay's for being too middle class – and failed. Given its

clientele it is not terribly expensive and has a very fine reputation. Amenities perfectly acceptable but disabled access difficult.

Cumberland Bar Cumberland Street *Chain*   G15

M-W 12pm-11.30pm, Th-S 12pm-12am, Sun 12.30pm-10pm
A well-equipped, modern traditional bar with small beer garden that is dedicated to serving a wide range of real beers in tip-top condition. Co-owned with Bow Bar.

The Wally Dug Northumberland Street *Managed* G17

M-S 12pm-1am, Sun 12.30pm-1am
Down steep stairs, this a quiet wee bar with decent beer – the name being Scots for China Dog.

The Newtown Bar Dublin Street *Free House*   G13

Sun-Th 12pm-1am, FS 12pm-2am
An excellent hostelry, catering for the slightly more mature end of the city's gay population.

Queen's Arms Frederick Street *Managed*   G4

M-S 11am-1am, Sun 12.30pm-1am
A grand wee traditional basement bar, with nice tiling and leaded glass, plus free finger food at five on Fridays. So Fred said.

Jekyll and Hyde Hanover Street *Managed*   G11

11am-1am all week
A Victorian Gothic palace with a macabre theme; interesting decor, a nice line in skeletons, they sell Spell Bites and Sadistic Sandwiches. Ouch!

The Howff Thistle Street *Chain*   G10

M-W 11am-11pm, Th 11am-12am, FS 11am-1am, Sun 12.30pm-11pm
This nice green pub, cosy and traditional in style, living up to its name – originally meaning a room in someone's home where drink was sold.

The World Thistle Street *Tenancy*   G9

M-S 12pm-1am, Sun closed
A real ale pub with a classy wood panelled decor, very like an old fashioned upmarket lounge bar.

WEST END / HAYMARKET

The area from the west end of Princes Street along Shandwick Place to Haymarket is known as the West End. This part of Edinburgh is a mix of offices and shops, with a variety of different styles of pubs as well as wine bars and restaurants. A prosperous part of the town, it doesn't have as many houses as other part of the city centre, but it retains much 18th and 19th Century elegance. By the time we reach the Haymarket, we are moving away from Georgian elegance towards later Victorian city developments, many of which were industrial, and the traditionally working class areas of Gorgie and Dalry. In this section is included the Port Hamilton Tavern, which adjoins a major 19th Century artery – The Union Canal. It is only now being redeveloped after many years of neglect. This is not really a part of the town which attracts the tourists, though around Haymarket there are many hotels and guest houses, and there are a handful of pubs well worth visiting.

Rutland No 1 Rutland St/Place *Managed*   H5

10am-1am all week, breakfasts served on Sundays.
This pub could fool the uninitiated into thinking it is Edwardian,
while in fact it is another example of retro-styling. Its use of

mirrors is very fine, and the seats at the windows overlooking the
end of the magnificent Princes Street give a great view of passing
city life. This is a bar that serves keg beers and lagers with a
dozen malt whiskies and the same number of wines to go with
food. Pub grub, of a good standard and extensive range, is
supplied from a restaurant upstairs and is available from 12pm-
8pm and till 6pm weekdays. Prices for food are fair while drinks
are expensive. With a mixed trade of shoppers, tourists and
some business people, it keeps busy and gets the weekend party
trade. A fine reconstruction. They have disabled toilets.

Ryan's Queensferry Street *Chain*   H2

M-S 7.30am-1am, Sun 12.30pm-1am
This large pub with its extensive glass frontage used to be a fruit
market. Today it is an example of what reconstruction can do.
Uniquely, they sell Dublin-brewed Guinness here as opposed to
the stuff made in London where the water is hard. The price is
worth it. Additionally they have two cask beers, premium lagers,
over 50 kinds of whiskies, a good range of bottled beers and a
couple of dozen wines. There are pub lunch and à la carte
menus, the latter, as one would expect, is not cheap. All food is
cooked in house, is available till 10.30pm every night and they
pride themselves on its quality. The drink prices too are
expensive, but this is an unashamedly upmarket boozer. The
glass fronted coffee-house bit does a roaring trade all week.
Catering for the over 21s only, this is a bit of a trendy place but
some of the touches are magnificent. Wisely they have retained
the hand-painted, fan-vaulted ceiling from the days of Rankin's
Fruit Market, and the swan in the dome behind the front door is
particularly fine. The designer has also added a nice touch with
the only solid brass bar top in the UK – beautiful, but a pain for
the staff who have to polish it. The location at the west end of
Princes Street ensures a steady clientele of shoppers, tourists and
a lot of business types in suits. They have a strict dress code,
and the bar staff themselves can be seen in waistcoats. Although
the glass front is a bit of a goldfish bowl and the Man from Fife
thought it a Poser' Paradise, this trendy and upmarket bar is well
run and very fine indeed. There is a saying that you get what you
pay for. Amenities fine and there is wheelchair access.

Mather's Queensferry Street *Managed*   H4

M-Th 11am-12am, FS 11am-1am, Sun 12.30pm-12am
Mather's has six cask ales, 107 malt whiskies and eight wines,
along with all the standard spirits and a good range of bottled
beers. It also has a reputation, built over many years, of being a

pub where the beer is of the best. Food consists of rolls and toasties but this is a bar where the drink and the 'craic' are very much the thing. Virtually everything in the one-roomed bar is listed, though the bar is not original. The fine gantry, like the tiled entrance, the cornices, the leaded glass windows and chandeliers, all stem from 1903 when the pub was opened by the original Hugh Mather. It has been a city fixture ever since, though there has been some tasteful restoration due to wear and tear. The decor echoes the traditional aspect of the bar to create a beautiful unitary feeling. This is primarily a traditional man's bar, with plenty of standing room as well as tables and chairs round the walls, though it must be said that women are not made to feel unwelcome. For a city centre pub it is remarkable in that about 80% of its custom is composed of regulars, though there is a steady stream of people who have read about Mather's in various drink guides, as well as shoppers and other passing trade. With its imposing frontage and general Edwardian magnificence, Mather's has been allowed to stick to being a traditional Scottish pub and for that the brewery are to be commended. This is a welcoming friendly place and there is always someone to talk to over a quiet pint. At the weekends they get some partygoers – of all ages. This could be described as the ultimate city centre meeting place. Fine old toilets are down steep stairs.

The Rat and Parrot Shandwick Place *Chain* H6

Sun-W 10am-11pm, Th 10am-12am, FS 10am-1am
This is part of a brewery owned chain, clearly derived from English traditional alehouses, that strongly features its food provision. Along a bar with a parallel seating area for food, they have a range of a dozen keg beers and lagers, lots of bottled beers and a wine list of ten, with two different kinds of fizz as well. Food is available from 10am-10pm and the idea is clearly to provide exactly the same sort of quality and service as in other similarly named establishments. We assume the name is meant to be amusing but do not understand why. Although the gantry is listed and is a fine one, the rest of the pub is pretty faceless, though clean and bright. The problem with places like this is that while they are efficient and make a lot of money, they suppress originality and local colour and could be anywhere from Land's End to John O' Groats. The assumption is that people like such homogenised fare as they can get here – it is virtually all brought in frozen and simply reheated and served – and as the prices are reasonable there may be a case. However as the Man from Fife would say; what's wrong with a bit of character, or a bit of originality, or with a bit of taste? Such chains stand out in a city

like Edinburgh, which despite the machinations of the big boys in
the bevvy trade still has a wonderful diversity of drinking and
eating establishments. The clientele in the Rat and Parrot seems
to be shoppers and tourists with a few local office staff attracted
by the decent prices. They attract a Friday 5 o'clock crowd – but
show me a pub that doesn't. Amenities are fine but too small for
wheelchairs.

Au Bar Shandwick Place *Managed*   H7

M-Th 11am-12am, FS 11am-1am, Sun 12pm-12am
There is nothing wrong with pubs having a theme. This is
extremely unusual in being modelled on the Paris Great Exhibition
of 1900. With beautiful turned wood, wrought iron rails on the
bar, and some very interesting tile mosaics, this is a tasteful and
comfortable bar that borders on the pretentious but escapes. The
painting of the Great Exhibition is a nice touch, as is the copper
bar and the use of glass throughout. They have two real ales at
fair city centre prices, ten malt whiskies and, strangely, only a few
wines. Food is upmarket pub grub with table service, available till
7pm during the week and 6pm on Fridays, but not at the
weekend. Prices are fair. Au Bar attracts a steady trade in
business lunchers and shoppers, tourists and other passing
trade. An interesting, quiet place popular with couples. Amenities
fine and good access.

Melville Lounge William Street *Managed*   H8

Sun-W 10am-11pm, Th-S 11am-12.30am
This is a pleasant, back street pub that claims to bring a touch of
the country inn to the city. With a couple of cask beers, half a
dozen malts and ten wines, the Melville does a good trade in
food from 12pm-3pm and 6pm-9pm. All home made, the menu is
traditional with new standards like chilli and Cajun chicken at
pretty fair prices. With lots of brocade chairs and wall seating, a
nice round bar, interesting old fashioned windows and a nice
selection of Edinburgh prints, the atmosphere is homely and
comforting. They attract a mix of people from local offices and
shops as well as tourists during the week. They have their own
regular trade in the evenings and at the weekends they entertain
a lot of couples. Not a place for the mad party-goer, but the
prices are very reasonable. Amenities fine but no disabled
access.

Bert's Bar William Street *Chain* H9

M-W 11am-11pm, Th-S 11am-12am, Closed most Sundays
This, the original Bert's (the other is in Stockbridge), is part of a
small chain owned by a bigger pub chain. With up to eight cask
ales on at any one time, at decent city centre prices, Bert's is
clearly aimed at the beer freak market. They carry a good range
of heritage bottled beers, enough of a variety of whiskies and
spirits and a wine list of six. Presumably the wines are to
complement the lunch menu, available from 12pm-2.30pm.
Perhaps not, however – as the main feature of the menu is pies,
and Bert's claim to make the best mince pies in town. The meat
pie was for many years the traditional working man's lunch in
pubs. It still survives in some bars and at some football grounds,
in its original form of lumps of greasy mutton wrapped in
cardboard. Bert's pies are nothing like those reminders of the
bad old days. They do a wide range of different fillings, including
some vegetarian. With soups, and even filled ciabatta, this is
traditional à la 21st Century. The bar is mock traditional,
tastefully done with a very fine gantry, originally from an
Edwardian site elsewhere, new leaded glass and a black marble
bar. The decor focuses round framed rugby club strips in the bar
and back room. With a weekday lunch time crowd of office staff
and shoppers, Bert's has a regular crowd, many of whom are
rugby supporters from all over the city. A wide range of board
games is kept behind the bar. They also attract tours, drawn by
the reputation for good beer. This is one city centre bar that can
be busier on a Friday than a Saturday night and is a place where
couples feel comfortable. Amenities fine but down stairs.

Caledonian Ale House Haymarket *Free House* H11

Sun-W 11am-12am, Th-S 11am-1am
With eight real beers (like most similar pubs including a variety of
guest ales in that number), a range of 24 malts and a reasonable
wine list, the Callie, as it likes to be called, is an upmarket beer
shop. It is a roomy, well-appointed bar, with some Edwardian
features like the tiled frieze and the cornices complemented by
modern subtle colours, subdued lighting and lots of flowers.
Behind the bar there are Doric columns round the till giving the
passing notion of a shrine to money – which is what a lot of bars
actually are. Lunch is on from 12pm-3pm every day and is
reasonably priced, while the beers are on the expensive side.
Seeing itself as sophisticated and mature, the Callie has no
entertainment but will have television sports from time to time,
and the re-introduction of live music is under consideration. This

is a pub where lots of the customers are couples. The day time crowd of office workers and shoppers is increased by a considerable input from the many local guest houses. With a fine long bar and lots of comfortable seating at tables, this is a friendly pub where the staff definitely have a sense of humour. Apart from calling the Man from Fife 'Sir', we were told that the staff can't stand rude customers ('but don't say the same about the staff!') Although no longer a jazz venue, this is still a bar for those who think themselves sophisticated drinkers. Amenities fine and accessible.

Ryrie's Bar Haymarket *Managed*   **H13**

M-S 11am-12am, Sun 12.30pm-12am
With three real ales in excellent condition, a range of keg and bottled beers and a dozen malts, this is very much a traditional working man's pub made good. They put on food from 11am-6.30pm; the quality is good and the prices very fair, as is the beer. The upstairs lounge is used for eating and can be hired. Being next door to the Haymarket Railway Station and a major road fork, they obviously get a lot of passing trade which includes locals, shoppers, office workers, football fans, travellers and Uncle Tom Cobbley and all. The magnificent Victorian frontage with its light coloured wood and glorious leaded glass is echoed inside, where all of the fittings are original or tastefully restored. The long bar with its brass foot rail and the gantry behind are models of their type, and you are aware of decades of drinkers having stood where you are as you sup your pint in Ryrie's. First built in 1862, it has been providing a good service since then and the customers will tell you how highly they rate the beer – without being asked, which is always a good sign. Music in the bar has long been a feature, currently on Thursdays and Sundays, with a tendency towards folk and/or AOR and it is a grand place to play. Long an attraction for visitors staying at the nearby hostel – some of whom have complimented your correspondent's clumsy fumblings, on the guitar – the mix continues to be cosmopolitan while retaining the feel of a traditional bar. It tends to get very busy on Saturdays when the Hearts are playing up the road at Tynecastle. The pub 5-a-side team are not worth mentioning, said Des. Amenities fine, but no disabled access.

Port Hamilton Tavern Fountainbridge *Free House*   **H12**

M-S 9am-1am, Sun 12.30pm-1am
Any city that makes a feature of its pub life needs to have a variety of types of bar, and the Port Hamilton Tavern is unique. The pub is housed in a small building still owned by the

Waterways Board. The Union Canal, which was once a major trade artery to Glasgow, ends behind the bar and is currently in the throes of being upgraded. This is the oldest pub in the area, dating from 1841. Although they only have keg beers and a few malts (a good variety at very low prices, admittedly) they do have something else. This is the home of Independence whisky, the brainchild of the man who ran this place till recently. The long, plainly decorated bar has an interesting line in both photographs and original oil paintings of Edinburgh scenes – which tourists are always disappointed to find are not for sale! The photographs show celebrities like Sean Connery being given bottles of Independence whisky, and it is a fact that this blend is ordered from all over the world when various ex-colonies celebrate the anniversary of their own independence (strangely, Independence whisky has not become a big seller in the United States so far). Clearly, this is a pub that is very nationalistic. It is pretty much a working class pub and it gets a lot of regulars and passing trade from the nearby bingo hall and bus stops. If this isn't the cheapest pub in Edinburgh it must be close, and if you can take the politics it is very welcoming indeed. Food, I was told, is limited to crisps with a fork. Amenities tolerable and accessible.

The Granary Queensferry Street *Managed*   **H3**

M-F 7.30am-1am, S 8am-1am, Sun 9am-1am
This interesting bar has some great tiling and lots of wood fixtures. Theres a bit of a rural feel about the place, and it features a wide range of food.

Haymarket Bar West Maitland Street *Managed*   **H10**

M-W 11am-12am, Th-S 11am-1am, Sun 11am-12am
Great, big, traditional-style pub that features live sport on television and opens a lot of hours.

Flares Hope Street *Managed*   **H1**

MT closed, W-Sun 4pm-1am
With swirling, flashing disco lights, this brash and bright boozer has a big bar floor area to strut your stuff in platform heels. 70's disco lives! Boogie on down!

West End Hotel Palmerston Place *Free House*   **H14**

M-S 11am-12am, Sun 12.30pm-12am
A very well known inner city sanctum for Gaels, with a strong music tradition, this place often feels like the ceilidh never stops.

SOPHISTICATED STOCKIE

Initially a village outside the city, Stockbridge has long had a distinctive bohemian cum bourgeois feel to it. St Vincent Street has a group of basement bars that have for a long time served as a focus for those wanting to go bar-hopping. Prices do vary here, but mainly they are on the high side. This is a prosperous part of the town with a good selection of local shops and several food specialists. With the Water of Leith flowing through it, Stockbridge retains something of a village feel; an atmosphere that is undoubtedly added to by the quality of many of the pubs here. Many city inhabitants like the odd Saturday afternoon in Stockbridge – it does have a lot to offer.

Dean Tavern Dean Street *Managed*   12

M-Th 11am-12am, FS 11am-12.30am, Sun 12.30pm-11pm
This square-shaped bar is owned and run by Scottish & Newcastle Breweries. All the beers are keg and there is a standard range of spirits. Food is limited to pizzas and other snacks from the freezer. Although it has been primarily a local bar for many years, its decor is again restored Victorian though plainer than most, and it is quite pleasant. It has a range of interesting prints on the walls and is one of those pubs whose sum is greater than its parts. The regular clientele includes many who have moved from the area – gentrification has seen

substantial population shifts out of the centre of Edinburgh – who think that the Dean is well worth a journey back for the friendly and familiar service. Prices are cheap for the area, and dominoes and darts are available for its sportier customers. Amenities fine.

St Bernard Bar Raeburn Place *Free House* 14

M-W 11am-12pm, Th-S 11am-1am, Sun 11am-11pm
This tiny wee bar in downtown Stockbridge is a clean and well-kept traditional local hostelry. Some of the fittings are original, but the bar has been extensively refurbished. The limited range of beer and lager is all keg, and there is nothing extraordinary about the range of spirits. The clientele is local and tends towards the elderly, which means a pretty steady stream of customers all day, gradually picking up from about 2pm. Like the staff, the customers are friendly and welcoming to strangers and passing trade. The word is that the place has much improved since a previous owner left. Amenities fine.

Bert's Bar Raeburn Place *Chain* 15

M-Th 11am-12am, FS 11am-1am, Sun 12.30pm-1am
This smart pub is part of a small chain which goes out of its way to cater to the real beer drinker. At any time they have 8 cask conditioned ales, always with a guest or two, and they are invariably in fine condition. They carry good selections of both malt whisky and wine. The food, available throughout the day, is cooked on the premises. Bert's Bars are noted particularly for their range of pies; which go well beyond the traditional Scottish parcel of grease, and include veggie and seafood varieties. The decor is repro-traditional and there are rooms at the back where local clubs and societies regularly gather. A friendly and informal sort of place, Bert's attracts a few office workers during the day and at nights brings in mainly local trade. At weekends, however, this clean, well-kept and welcoming place gets very busy. Amenities are fine and accessible.

Maison Hector Deanhaugh Street *Managed* 16

M-Th 11am-12am, F 11am-12am, S-Sun 10.30am-1am
Some pubs are simply unique. Although elsewhere I have drawn attention to the lack of imagination in so many brewery-owned pubs, there is no lack of imagination here. The effect of the place is instantaneous as you come in through the revolving door. With an eclectic, almost anarchic mixture of styles that includes velvet and wrought iron, stained glass panels, a phenomenal wine rack behind the bar and a strong echo of the wilder artistic styles of

Barcelona, Maison Hector is definitely one of a kind. With no real ales on offer, they do have a very good range of wines, along with pub food that originates in the restaurant kitchen at the back. Available till late, it shouldn't really be called pub grub at all and includes a fair range of veggie dishes. They open early at the weekends for coffee and breakfast. Although at first glance very trendy, the clientele is in fact quite mixed, with all ages, quite a few regulars and a lot of weekend trade. Newspapers are available, and during the day a fair amount of office trade is in evidence. Sunday afternoons and Thursday evenings they have live jazz/blues – a very civilised touch. Even with its Mediterranean influences, high quality food and definite café-bar ambience, Maison Hector manages to avoid being twee – the bar staff are helpful and friendly. The Man from Fife, though growling about the place being too foreign for Edinburgh, had to be dragged screaming from the bar. Distinctive and interesting, Maison Hector places an emphasis on high-class service so it is not cheap. Wheelchair access is problematic, but they see their gents toilet as a feature – it certainly is.

Hamilton's of Stockbridge Hamilton Place *Managed* 17

M-W 11.30am-12am, Th-S 11.30am-1am, Sun 12.30pm-11.30pm
This is a big, well-appointed, traditional style brewery pub that has had recent renovation, as usual stressing the Victorian hey-day of pub design. As the original Hamilton's opened in 1834 this seems fair enough. With a handful of real ales, a fair selection of spirits and a menu of burgers and baked potatoes on till nine, it is a pretty standard brewery offering. Added value are in the four pint jugs on offer at cut price, clearly aimed at the predominantly young and student clientele they have targeted here. A few older locals can still be spotted. Again, as is common, all big sports events are featured on the big screen, but they also throw in quiz and karaoke nights. With a steady trade all week this an efficiently run hostelry that gets very busy at the weekends. Amenities acceptable.

The Bailie St Stephen Street *Free House* 18

M-S 11am-12.30am, Sun 11am-11pm
This well known pub, at the corner of Kerr Street and St Stephen Street, in the centre of Stockbridge, is a basement bar like a few others nearby. Its dark exterior is matched inside, where there is a dark central bar surrounded by wall seating and tables. The lighting is subdued and this, coupled with a unusually attentive staff, make the atmosphere quite relaxed. Beyond the bar is a fair sized seating area adjoining the kitchen, where the restaurant style food is prepared till the early evening. The Bailie sees itself

as a bit plush and posh, and the Man from Fife was heard to mutter something that sounded like 'Poser's Paradise'. This is perhaps a bit unfair as the Bailie does have lot going for it, though it is fair to say the clientele are adult and a bit up-market. They have a few real ales, a good selection of malt whiskies and wines, and fine coffee; this is an expensive place. The clientele is quite mixed, with well-off locals rubbing shoulders with officers of the local constabulary and a range of shopkeepers – the area has a mixture of interesting shops inherited from its days as a hippy shopping ghetto. The general atmosphere is much like that of an old-fashioned lounge bar; no sign of anyone in working clothes other than suits! Over the years it has seen a fair number of artists, musicians and literary figures crossing its threshold. One particular attraction is that there is no canned music or juke box – the only sounds are those of the day to day functioning of a good, well run pub – bliss! Decent amenities but the bar is inaccessible to wheelchairs.

The Watershed St Stephen Street *Free House* 19

10am-1am All week
This modern basement bar is open for coffee and food from 10 am all week; it is very much one of the new café-bars that are becoming the in-thing. It is a Mediterranean style place with bright and light decor and fittings and a steel bar. Drinks consist of premium lagers, the odd explosive cider, a range of bottled beers and a fair selection of wines and spirits. As one would expect, cocktails and other mixtures are available. The food is high-class for a pub and available throughout the day until the evening. The clientele is varied and leans towards the younger end the scale, with regulars, some students and quite a few business people. The friendly and efficient staff told me they liked to drink there on days off – always a recommendation, of sorts. Amenities fine given the usual problems of basement bars.

The Antiquary St Stephen Street *Free House* I10

M-W 11.30am-12.30am, Th-S 11.30am-1am, Sun 11am-12am
This largish basement bar in St Stephen Street has recently undergone a major refurbishment that seems to have done little to alter the atmosphere while increasing the efficiency of service. Divided into two main areas with booths and small rooms off, there is a smallish bar serving both main rooms. The decor is no more than standard traditional reproduction – with lots of wood, some leaded glass, and prints on the wall. They stock only keg beers, a generally standard range of spirits (with the odd brain-scrambler like absinthe featured) and do 1/3 bottle glasses of wine

at a temptingly reasonable price. Food, cooked on the premises, is
fine and available through to early evening, and on Sundays they
open for breakfast at 11am – a service now quite common but which
started here. The problem is, arriving for breakfast and having one's
choice of all the Sunday press, can lead one into a state of leisure
that all too suddenly sees 'just the one drink' leading to a sudden
feeling of 'where did the afternoon go?'. They also do Saturday
breakfasts – doubling the danger. The owner, Andy, makes no qualms
about this being the scene of some serious drinking and reckons his
clientele is both eclectic and bohemian. He sees The Antiquary as
part of the inherited Stockbridge hippy tradition. They hold a folk
session on Thursday evenings, continuing a long-standing
commitment to acoustic music in The Antiquary. This is also one of
those Edinburgh pubs that lay claim to a ghost; a female who has
been seen on several occasions by unaccompanied members of
staff. Because of the very steep stairs, entry can be difficult – exit
can be even more so. Otherwise the amenities are fine.

St Vincent Bar St Vincent Street *Chain*   I11

M-S 11am-12am, Sun 12.30pm-11pm
Although recently refurbished, much of the wood and leaded
glass in this classic Victorian style bar is in fact original, as are
some of the prints and mirrors on the wall. Having started life as
a pub after the First World War, this bar has a commitment to
real ale of which a goodly selection is always available. The
magnificent original gantry contains a fine selection of malts and
they also provide wickedly strong Scrumpy (cider) and a range of
boutique beers. They occasionally stock a specially featured
selection of cask conditioned ales. No food is served other than
snacks. There is a pool table at the back of this fine wee bar, but
they have no live music, nor thankfully, a juke box. The clientele
is always mixed with students, workers, locals and suits all
mingling freely. Amenities fine and accessible.

Raeburn Hotel Raeburn Place *Managed*   I1

M-F 9am-12am, S-Sun 9am-1am
Although technically a hotel, the Raeburn has made many a
family's afternoon since opening up its refreshing beer garden.
For many favours much thanks.

Macandrew's Dean Street *Chain*   I3

M-S 11am-11pm, Sun 12.30pm-11pm
If you like a pint and a game of darts or pool in decent
surroundings, you could do worse than drop in to this very
Scottish pub.

BROUGHTON / CANONMILLS /
TOP OF THE WALK

Edinburgh's New Town is one of the architectural wonders of the world. It was initially conceived as one of the first instances of modern city planning in the late 18th Century when Edinburgh was one of the leading centres of the Enlightenment. Today the New Town retains much of its Georgian magnificence. Primarily a residential area – of broad streets with big houses for the gentry and smaller streets with smaller apartments for the artisans and servants – the New Town does have a few streets which were given over to shops and pubs. We have covered some of the pubs in this area in the Stockbridge section. Here we are looking primarily at the area to the east of the New Town which encompasses Broughton Street, Canonmills and the top of Leith Walk; a famous old street disgracefully treated over the past two decades by politicians who claim to represent the interests of the city's inhabitants. Our chosen area also includes the magnificence of the east end of Princes Street and the somewhat shabbier area of Abbeyhill.

Apart from the architectural monstrosity that the British Government chose to erect on the site of the old St James Square, the site opposite it at the top of Leith Walk has been allowed to lie waste for many years – while keeping up the profits of the developers because of an underground car park. One of the central areas of one of the planet's finest cities is thus abused. Despite the planning blight and obvious indifference of our politicians to the actuality, rather than the image of the city, the area has retained some fine old pubs, while others have been renovated to surprisingly high standards. Our Man from Fife, never a fan of politicians, has been known to suggest drastic action – but his inability to locate a guillotine stopped him in his tracks.

Robbie's Leith Walk *Chain*   **J18**

M-F 12pm-12am, S 11am-12am, Sun 12.30pm-12am
Basically a plain working class type boozer half way down Leith walk, this is a pub with a reputation. With six cask ales and two dozen malts on offer, along with everything else, this is a grand place for people who like their beer. They do not stoop to serving food but stick to two attractions – drink and good conversation. The conversation is brisk and very much of the Scottish sarcastic school, so the Man from Fife was among friends. The customers will freely express their praise for the place given half a chance – even the sober ones. An old pub, Robbie's was extensively enlarged and refurbished a good few years ago. It is a big, roomy, welcoming howff with lots of wood in the traditional style, nice prints and mirrors and a real mixter-maxter of stuff above the gantry – including a stuffed badger, fox and some kind of bird, thought to be a goose. Although tending towards a male clientele, they attract a fair sprinkling of couples and women, and increasingly students, who are just discovering the area. The prices are high for the location, but Robbie's is seen by its customers as a cut above the rest of the local bars. This isn't exactly pretentious as they were recently mentioned in a New York literary magazine, whose correspondent dropped in hoping to find Irvine Welsh of *Trainspotting* fame, and his literary pals – none of whom are actually that regular. The Hibernian FC stadium is just along the road so this is very much Hibee country. The pub team, Robbie's Raiders, have been winning the local pub football league for quite a few years. Nuff said. They have disabled toilets.

Conan Doyle York Place *Managed* J11

M-Th 11am-12am, FS 11am-1am, Sun 1pm-12am
This pub is certainly one a kind. Whoever first thought of the idea
of the theme pub would love this bar. Situated on the corner of
the fine Georgian York Place, the Conan Doyle has been
deliberately created with the aim of being as close to Sherlock
Holmes' drawing room as possible. Holmes' creator, Sir Arthur
Conan Doyle, was born opposite the pub in Picardy Place where a
statue of him now stands. The pub, which can only be accessed
up steep sets of stairs, is a wonder of mock Victoriana. Tasselled
curtains, sofas and armchairs are covered in velvet and an
imitation carved fireplace is complete with imitation coal fire.
Original it isn't but with its air-conditioning and central heating, it
is comfortable at all times of the year. The drinks on offer are a
bit unexceptional with keg beers, a couple of premium lagers and
a dozen or so malt whiskies. They also stock alcopops and do a
range of cocktails for the more sophisticated palate. The menu is
standard brought in pub grub; mainly sizzlers and snacks. Food is
available from 12-10pm during the week, till 3pm on a Friday, 5pm
on a Saturday and from 12-5 pm on Sunday. Prices, like the beer,
are reasonable this close to the city centre. As one would expect
this is a pub that attracts a lot of tourists, some of them Sherlock
Holmes devotees. All year round at lunch and as the offices and
shops close it attracts a lot of workers from that nearby atrocity,
the St James Shopping Centre, and a steady stream of shoppers
too. At the weekends it is very busy and tends to attract a pre-club
younger crowd. Not really anything special other than its theme.
Amenities fine. No disabled access at all.

Mather's Bar Broughton Street *Managed* J10

M-Th 11am-12.30am, FS 11am-1am, Sun 12.30pm-11pm
This pub often gets confused with the other Mather's near the
West End of Princes Street but, although a fair enough pub, it is
not in the same class as its namesake. They stock 5 cask ales
and make a feature of their malt whisky selection with over a
hundred, including old and rare malts. This brings in interested
tourists and tipplers. Prices are fair for a city centre location. The
pub is on two floors – making access difficult for the toilets – and
is in mock Edwardian style. Food, which is a combination of
frozen and kitchen cooked is reasonably priced and available 12-
10pm all week. The clientele is a mix of shoppers and office
staff during the day with more locals in the evening. This is a pub
where you'll see media people but with none of the usual
pretentiousness. Amenities fine.

Baroque Bar Broughton Street *Tenancy*   J9

M-S 11am-1am, Sun 12.30pm-1am
With three cask ales, premium lagers, cocktails, pitchers and
shooters, and a wine list of a dozen, the Baroque Bar sets out
to cater for a wide range of tastes. Although at the expensive
end of the range and very much a modern "style" bar, this is not
one that sees its customer base as solely the young. The decor
is quite unusual with flashing Christmas-tree lights over the bar
and ceiling, copper covered toilet doors, more copper on the bar
light shades and some odd bits of free form bar architecture.
Add in the bright almost Mediterranean colours, trendy wrought
iron screens and chairs, and some judicious (some not) use of
tile mosaic and you could almost sense the influence of the
great Catalan architect Gaudi. It may be a bit more gaudy than
Gaudi, but none the worse for that. The feeling is bright and fun –
and this atmosphere is actively encouraged by the young staff.
The Man from Fife, a closet art-freak, was taken by the tiled
mirror on the north wall – luckily it wasn't taken by him! They
serve a range of food from 11am-10pm from Sunday to
Thursday, and till 8pm on Friday and Saturday. Prices are not
cheap but the quality is fine. The clientele is a mix of people
ranging from their 20s to mid 40s and includes a lot of passing
trade – local office and shop workers come in at lunchtimes
and early evenings. The Baroque Bar is a relaxed place to have
a drink on your own, whatever your sex or age. At weekends
this bright and trendy establishment attracts quite a lot of
pre-clubbers. They have disabled toilets.

The Barony Bar Broughton Street *Managed*   J8

M-Th 11am-12am, FS 11am-12.30am, Sun 12.30pm-11pm
It is amazing how well breweries can manage pubs – when the
law prevents them playing around with them! This is a listed late
Victorian bar which stocks a selection of seven real ales, a
couple of premium lagers, a range of heritage bottled beers, 20
malt whiskies and a decent wine list of a dozen or so. Prices are
mid-range for the city centre and food is supplied daily from
11am-9pm except on Sundays, though they will supply pies at all
times. The menu is standard pub grub with a twist, some brought
in and some cooked in the little kitchen off the bar. Prices are
reasonable rather than good. This is a pub with a real eclectic
mix of customers: students, locals, office workers, passing
shoppers and a smattering of creative people. The office crowd
tend to cluster at lunch and after work while later it is more of a
local pub. The real star is the Barony itself. With beautiful tiling

inset with painted landscapes hidden by modern benches, things are not all as they should be! The original long gantry and bar are fine examples of the bar designer's craft and at the short section of this L-shaped bar there is a coal fire. The bar still has original working brass water taps. On Sundays the Barony puts on live music which tends towards classic rock and pop songs rather than folk. This is definitely not a football pub and there is no sign of a big screen. All in all this is a good example of what a traditional Edinburgh Victorian pub was really like – and the atmosphere is pretty good too. The toilets are accessible for disabled people.

The Phoenix Broughton Street *Free House*   J7

M-S 8am-1am, Sun 12.30pm-1am
Sometimes appearances can be deceptive. The Phoenix looks a bit run down from the outside but is a well run establishment on two levels, with a couple of cask ales, seven or eight malt whiskies and a range of keg beers. The prices are good for the area and they overcome the lack of food on offer by encouraging their customers to frequent the local delicatessen two doors up! The Phoenix features a lot of television sport and the clientele is mostly male, but it certainly isn't a place where a woman would be made to feel uncomfortable. Hooray Henry students can be seen at the bar talking to local workmen and it is this mix that The Phoenix thrives on. Downstairs is Harley's Lounge where at the weekends they have a DJ and the decor merges strange murals with Stone Age Cave paintings in an intriguing fashion. Amenities fine but no disabled access.

The Cask and Barrel Broughton St *Chain*   J5

M-W 11am-12.30am, Th-S 11am-1am, Sun 12.30pm-12.30am
This is a highly successful recent renovation modelled on what passes for a traditional pub these days – lots of wood and an ornate gantry – here it certainly works. With six regular cask ales and up to four guests, this is a place for the dedicated beer drinker, featuring Czech beers and German Weissbier. They also stock a range of 40+ malt whiskies. Nestling at the back of the beer shelf are a few bottles of the deceptively powerful Lindisfarne Mead, made by monks in northern England and to be treated with respect, if not caution. Given its location in the prosperous New Town and its proximity to the centre of the city, the prices can only be described as very reasonable. Food is served from 12pm-2pm and consists of a home made main dish and soup, both cooked on the premises. Other than that the menu is limited to filled rolls and toasted sandwiches. The

U-shaped bar serves a large wooden-floored area with old barrels and tables with chairs round the walls. Dedicated to the serving of good beer, the service is highly efficient, even when the bar is at its most hectic. This brings in a regular crowd from over a very wide area of the city. In addition they have a fair amount of passing trade and a few tourists from nearby guest houses. That there are not more tourists is perhaps partly due to the surprising fact that the Cask is not included in the current Good Beer Guide. The Cask caters to the sport on telly crowd and can get very busy indeed. The crowd is generally quite mixed and tends towards the cosmopolitan. Disabled toilets.

The Stag's Head Broughton Road *Free House*   J4

M-S 11am-1am, Sun 12.30pm-1am
This traditional local pub on two levels sells the standard range of keg beers and has a selection of 20 malts on its fine, wee, original gantry. A fair sized pub, the Stag's Head does no food and is pretty reasonably priced. The decor retains some of its original Edwardian features, such as cornices and plasterwork ceiling. The bar, too, looks original. The walls have interesting old prints and photographs as well as original bar mirrors. The clientele are primarily local people, though they also attract some passing trade. It is noticeable that the patrons are of all ages and during the day primarily male. This doesn't stop some of the bar staff suggesting a better name for the place might be Cupid's. They have a great ladies darts team – local champions for the past 10 years. Amenities fine and accessible.

Smithie's Bar Eyre Place *Chain*   J3

11am-12.30am all week – open for Sunday breakfast
With half a dozen real beers at very competitive prices, and two dozen malts, this deliberately antique, smallish pub has a style all its own. They do in-house food at lunchtimes and Sunday brunch. The menu comprises of good pub standards at reasonable prices. The style is cod-Victorian verging on the kitsch, and quite amusing. Although less than a couple of decades old, they are the only pub in Edinburgh to have gas lighting! The painted mirrors are a feature, with flowers and birds, but do remember taste is a very personal thing. The clientele is a mixed bag including couples, telly sports fans, some local office staff and a modicum of passing trade. Smithie's might look a bit like a film set for a Jack the Ripper film, but it is comfortable and welcoming. Amenities fine, but no disabled facilities.

Northern Bar Howard Place/Inverleith Row *Chain*   **J1**

11am-12am all week, breakfasts on Sunday
With five cask ales, ten malts and a list of ten wines, the
Northern Bar is at first sight another traditional Edinburgh bar
from the turn of the last century. However, about the only original
bits left are the leaded glass doors you enter through. This is a
big roomy pub with a back room used extensively for big screen
sports. They put on a range of food from 12pm-7pm daily,
some of which is cooked in-house. With a lunch and tea time clientele
drawn from nearby offices – people need a place to come and
smoke a cigarette it seems – they have a steady weekday trade.
This picks up in the summer with visitors going to the nearby
Botanic Gardens bringing in a lot of trade. Popular with couples,
the Northern gets busier at the weekends. No disabled toilets.

The Windsor Buffet Elm Row (Leith Walk) *Managed* **J16**

M-Th 11am-11.45pm, FS 11am-12.45am, Sun 12.30pm-11.45pm
This fine fronted bar has two cask ales and two dozen malts,
standard bottled beers and spirits. The Windsor also stocks half
a dozen wines. Food here is restricted to frozen snacks, but is
served all day. Famous in the past for its home-cooking and
showbiz buzz – next door was a theatre and then a television
studio till a few years back – the Windsor is now primarily a
thriving local pub that gets a bit of passing trade. The pub itself
has a wealth of Victorian detail, from the long bar to cornice
work, small booths and rooms and some stunning stuff on the
walls. The doors and windows are all original leaded glass, with
the odd repair where necessary. The raised seating area at the
back can be all too comfortable. Apart from some delightful
photographs from Scottish Music Hall days, there is a truly
magnificent 19th Century Robert Burns poster behind the
armchairs near the Gents. The mix is eclectic, with working men
and women, professionals, artists, writers and musicians all
chatting at the bar, and a sprinkling of Dundee accents here and
there. It is a bar that has its own football team, mainly gentleman
just out of their teens (their umpteens); though word has it the
last time they won was during the war. Whether that was the
Second World War or the Boer War is not clear. The occasional
music policy has seen some fine nights, but the sight of swing
saxophonists strutting along the bar has sadly gone now. With
next door re-opening as a college film and television centre,
changes are probably afoot. The toilets are perfectly fine but
narrow doorways make wheelchair access a problem. The
manager is a Hun.

Maclachlan's Ale House Canonmills *Free House*   J2

M-Th 11am-12am, FS 11am-1am, Sun 12.30pm-12am
Good selection of real ale in this bright new version of a fine old
pub, the Coach Inn, that had the last water-engine driven beer
pumps in the city.

Bellevue Bar London Street *Chain*   J6

Sun-Th 12pm-1am, FS 11am-1am
For a long time a quiet and friendly if undistinguished bar, it is
about to come out with a new face. Toilets not recommended for
sleeping in, as the Man from Fife can testify.

CC Bloom's Leith Walk *Tenancy*   J12

6pm-3am all week
Used to be a bikers pub with a popular pool room, now
transmogrified into a gay bar which gets lots of custom,

Planet Out Leith Walk *Managed*   J13

M-F 4pm-1am, S-Sun 2pm-1am
Another one of the handful of gay bars in this area that seem to
do a steady trade. Modern and bright, loud and sassy.

Elm Bar Elm Row *Managed*   J14

M-Th 11am-12am, FS 11am-1am, Sun 12.30pm-11pm
Another traditional-style bar that doesn't always look after its real
beers as well as it might. Always busy.

JPs Elm Row *Managed*   J15

MT 11am-11pm, WTh 11am-12am, FS 11am-1am, Sun 11am-
11pm
Another brewery pub that is basically a local community pub but
brings in the tourists, with all day food and tables outside in the
summer sun.

The Old Salt Leith Walk *Managed*   J17

M-F 5am-11.30pm, S 5am-12am, Sun 12.30pm-11.30pm
Open early for shift workers, the Salt is a friendly bar that has
some interesting decorative touches on the nautical theme.

SUNNY LEITH

For centuries, there was rivalry between the people of Leith and those of Edinburgh. Leith has always been a seaport with all the associated industries and obvious vices, whereas Edinburgh, home of governance, the law and finance has always considered itself genteel. Its vices have tended to be hidden. Earlier this century the two were united, recognising the fact that physical distinctions had long since been absorbed in urban sprawl. The differing architectural styles of the two do however remain. In recent years, with the decline of shipping, Leith has become gentrified along its once notorious shores and now boasts a plethora of restaurants, café-bars, loft apartments and all the appurtenances of yuppiedom. The developments continue, with the location of the Scottish Office, now the administration of the new Scottish Executive, in the staggeringly ugly and inappropriate building at Victoria Quay. Do architects ever get over playing with lego as children? Further to this the Royal Yacht Britannia now resides in Leith and the area has begun to attract tourists, while in the back streets poverty still exists as it always has done. In general, though, it has improved and, as it contains many of the oldest pubs in the combined city, is well worth a visit. Again, there is great variety of choice and for the most part the people are friendly – not something that has always been said of the native tribes of Edinburgh. Our trip round Sunny Leith, so known since an album by those most bespectacled and Scots of popsters, the Proclaimers, was entitled Sunshine over Leith, starts us down near the docks. It takes us on towards the major thoroughfare up to Edinburgh, Leith Walk, and back down towards the Shore. The opening hours in Leith tend to be earlier than most Edinburgh pubs and if you fancy a drink first thing in the morning, or are still up from the night before, this is the place to go.

The Shore Bar The Shore *Free House*   K1

M-S 11.30am-12pm, Sun 12.30pm-1am
Overlooking the Water of Leith as it merges with the waters of the River Forth, the Shore is a fine place incorporating a nice bar and a restaurant. The bar stocks four real ales, 20 malts and a substantial wine list, which one would not really call cheap. The wine list leans heavily towards French and New World wines, so no Buckfast here then. They serve a full restaurant menu in the bar from 12pm-2.30pm (3pm on a Sunday) and 6.30pm-10pm, giving the place a bistro-ish air. The menu is extensive and expensive for a pub, though not for a restaurant, and leans towards seafood and tapas. The interesting circular doorway (impossible for wheelchairs), brings you into a small, dark bar with lots of wood panelling, including the ceiling. The coal fires in both bar and restaurant make this a welcoming spot in winter, while in summer, tables outside attract a steady trade especially on sunny weekends – which are sadly unforeseeable in Scotland. This is a bar where the old-fashioned idea that candles on the tables lends an air of sophistication has never faded. The Shore regards itself as a kind of upmarket, professional classes watering hole, where the sophisticated bohemian might feel at home. This might be right, though where the Man from Fife and I could fit into that is anybody's guess. At the weekends they have some local trade, and with the gentrification of Leith there are more and more recent arrivals to the area who will like the Shore. Not as much of a Poser's Paradise as one might think. They regularly have jazz on Tuesday nights and daily during the Jazz Festival. Amenities fine but no disabled access.

The King's Wark The Shore *Tenancy*   K4

12pm-11pm all week
Wark is Scots for work; in this case referring to the building, which was put up as part of a complex in the early years of the

17th Century by the then king, James VI, before he deserted Scotland for bigger things in London. He installed tennis courts here and it seems it was bit of a retreat from Holyrood up the road. Whoever said bigger is better? At a later date the building was used as a plague hospice, and the historicity of the place is obvious, if not overwhelming. Inside, the bar has been refurbished on several occasions but still retains some original stone features, and the use of wood is very traditional. This is a place where the staff reckon there is an atmosphere even when it is empty, which given the history is hardly surprising. They stock four cask ales, 14 malt whiskies and a wine list of 40, which is there to support the food, for which they are well known and praised by their competitors. Food is available till 10pm, like all Leith eateries there is a seafood bias and it is reasonably priced for the quality. There is nothing pub grubby about it. With such an emphasis placed on food, the Wark attracts a lot of business lunch types – and Leith is full of advertisers, designers, accountants and other people of dubious provenance. There is not a plethora of suits and ties in the Wark, though it is very much a credit card crowd rather than a cash crowd. In the evenings it attracts a regular clientele, many of whom see this as a trendy place for trendy people, but the crowd is hardly teenaged. No music, no fruit machines and no juke box, definitely. Amenities fine but no disabled access.

The Malt and Hops The Shore *Free House*   K5

M-W 12pm-11pm, Th 12pm-12am, FS 12pm-1am, Sun 12pm-11pm

Another old Leith pub that has undergone a bit of a sea change, this used to be a good local club, a place the constabulary kept their eye on and a hangout for people of strange habits. Nowadays, this lovely square bar is a cracker. With eight cask ales, the dreaded cask conditioned cider (the very sight of this causes the Man from Fife to take deep breaths, then several pints of it) and an excellent range of over 50 malt whiskies and other spirits. They pride themselves on quality and service here. They also stock that most Scottish of beers, Fraoch, made from heather flowers! Food is available from 12pm-2pm, including Sunday breakfast and, though not as trendy as other nearby establishments, good, pub grub standard fare is cooked on the premises. Prices are mid-range for the area. Another pub with a coal fire, this low-ceilinged room is very welcoming indeed, with its scattering of tables and chairs and a fine wooden bar with a gantry about a century old. The building itself went up in 1745. The decor is fun, with beer mats, proprietary water jugs and glasses, interspersed with old prints and original bar mirrors on the walls and hanging from the original rafters. There is no juke box or fruit machine and the television only goes on for very special occasions. The Malt and Hops thrives on a regular trade of beer drinkers, local office workers at lunchtimes and early evenings, and the usual Shore-hoppers who come down here at the weekends. They like to think that all developments here are customer led, and hold the odd distinction of being the Gordon's Gin 'Scottish Gin and Tonic Pub of the Year 1999'! Fine amenities but no disabled access.

Cameo Bar Sandport Street *Chain*   K3

12pm-1am all week
Located close to the new government buildings at Victoria Quay, this is a bar attached to a restaurant. With two real beers and 12 malts, they do lots of beer promotions and are generally at the cheaper end of Leith's trendy bars. A bright modern pub on two levels, with a small oblong bar, the back room is used for sports TV stuff. Food is brought in from the Camargue restaurant next door, and is available throughout the day and evening. They have a beautiful tiled fireplace for their coal fire. The Cameo attracts a mix of tourists, office workers and some locals. Late at night, many of the staff from other bars and restaurants in the area drop in. At the weekends the crowd is younger, but generally they reckon their regulars are all ages. A friendly and efficient bar, its amenities are fine but there is no disabled access.

Carriers' Quarters Bernard Street *Free House*   K7

M-W 11am-11pm, Th 11am-12am, FS 11am-1am, Sun 11am-11pm
Some pubs simply reek of history. The Carriers has been the same basic shape since opening as a pub in 1785. With a small bar, a tiny snug and a delightful back room, this low-ceilinged and welcoming bar has changed its name on many occasions, but has now reverted to its original nomenclature. They stock six cask ales at a time, have 20 or so malt whiskies and a reasonable wine list. Prices are good for the area and they have a Happy Hour from 4pm-7pm, which pleased our Fife friend. Reasonably priced food is on at lunchtimes, and is all cooked in the tiny kitchen. The clientele is a mixed bag with locals, 5 o'clock and lunchtime suits and people attracted by the beer. The wee snug is an interesting nook where 'ladies of the night' used to sit awaiting custom. The trade continues, as in all ports, but these days it is on the streets and under tight police supervision – called high tolerance. The lovely stone-walled back room with its original fireplace and, yes, candles on the tables, plays host to blues music on Thursdays and attracts a decent crowd – a big

crowd would be impossible. A very attractive and friendly wee pub, the Carriers gets a good weekend trade and attracts a lot of couples. A friendly place where good humour is evident, they might have gone too far in the gents. In the trough, gentleman are encouraged to empty their pockets of change once they have emptied their bladders! Once the wire cage in the trough is full, the coins are washed and given to charity. Are they taking the piss or what? Access to such a notable bog is a bit difficult.

The Burns Alehouse Bernard Street *Free House*   K8

M-S 11am-11pm, Sun 11am-11pm. Open for coffees and breakfasts.

This pub is clearly named and themed after Robert Burns, Scotland's greatest ever poet (there is no argument, believe me – or else). His statue stands in the middle of Bernard Street. The Burns is a sophisticated, smallish bar that feels no need to follow tradition. Much like a 1950s bar with square wooden panels and mirrors, it is sparklingly clean and tidy. The Victorian mirror over the gantry is wonderfully original. Drinks on offer include four, and sometimes five real ales, 45 malt whiskies, a small handful of wines and a classic rum – Gosling's from Bermuda, at 75.5% alcohol by volume, not a drink for the fainthearted. Upstairs they have a restaurant and food is available in the bar 12pm-2pm and 6pm-9pm. Prices are very reasonable, and the menu is Scottish derived with a twist. They feature rosti, a form of Swiss potato cake; any place that dares to present haggis and neeps with rosti certainly shows confidence. With some of Burns' poems on the walls and set in table tops, the motif is carried so far that the bar staff are prepared to recite a poem or sing a Burns song on request. Smashing idea that. Although on the sophisticated side, this is a local, not a style bar and attracts a real mix of customers. These include workers from the docks over the road, office workers, local people and some tourists. Although space at the bar is limited and table seating necessary, they attract all ages here. This is a place that I am sure Burns would love – being a man who liked good pubs. Amenities fine but there is no disabled access.

Noble's Constitution Street *Chain*   K9

M-Th 11am-12.30pm, FS 11am-1.30am, Sun 10am-12.30am. Open for breakfasts.

Many pubs in Edinburgh and Leith have gone through a few changes. At one point, Nobles's was best known for putting on strippers, with rumours of all kinds of dubious activities. The magnificent painted plasterwork and leaded glass windows of the frontage are matched by a great hall of a room inside that retains many features from its days as a Victorian drinking palace; wooden fittings, leaded and stained glass panels, ornate plasterwork. Though the bar has been moved from its old central location, it has been tastefully refurbished. The nautical connections of Leith are celebrated with prints and photographs of various ships, models of sailing ships, an original and extremely loud ship's bell at the end of the bar and, round the corner from the bell, a plasterwork King Neptune in a position of honour. The light shining through the leaded and stained glass windows can make this place a delight on a sunny Leith day. Drinkers are catered for with a range of six to eight cask ales, a couple of dozen malts, sufficient rum and a growing wine list. Prices are at the upper end for Leith. They have in house pub grub at lunchtimes, 12pm-3pm and 10am-5pm on Sunday. The clientele is typically Leith, with sailors and dockers, office-workers, designers and advertising executives, local residents and a few tourists. This is a female friendly bar and a growing number of women drop in for a bevvie, singly and in groups – changed days for Noble's indeed! There is a proper stage and they put on blues-tinged music on Friday and Saturday nights, with an open mike 'party-piece' session on Thursdays. Weekends are hectic. Amenities fine and accessible.

Port O' Leith Constitution Street *Managed*   K10

M-S 8.30am-1am, Sun 12.30pm-1am
Open from early morning for shift workers and sailors from the docks, this is a wee pub with a big reputation. Sailors like this place and there is a steady regular local crowd who, along with the bar staff, are famous for making everyone welcome. They have one cask ale, half a dozen malts and a standard range of bottled beers and spirits. The decor is nautical, the roof a resplendent riot of different ship's flags, donated by customers who have sampled the delights of the Port. These flags come from big ships, little ships, coastal steamers, container ships, submarines and every kind of vessel afloat. The ship's figurehead opposite the bar smiles benignly on the prints and photographs of a similar range of vessels covering the walls. If you are in luck there might be a few rolls or sandwiches available, but this is pub where it seems the party rarely stops. The clientele consists of sailors, local residents and some passing trade, and it has been known for some serious drinking to take place here – many people who, having been in once, just keep coming back. When there are street fairs or other events on, this is the place to be, if you can get in. They do have a juke box and will occasionally

bring in entertainment for specific parties. When I was last in I
met a sailor at the bar, at 11.30 in the morning, who said he had
been a regular for 20 years and lived in the South of England
when he wasn't on board ship. He thought of the Port as a home
from home. Down to earth and unpretentious it may be, ordinary
it is not. Amenities are adequate but no proper disabled access.

Slammers Queen Charlotte Street *Free House*   K11

M-Th 6am-11pm, FS 6am-1am, Sun 12.30pm-1am
Like many local Leith community pubs, this is one that has lots
of hours to service its steady custom. With keg beers, ten malts
and the usual suspects in bottles and spirits, Slammers draws
people in with a Happy Hour from 12pm-8pm daily! It has a
predominantly male clientele and it is a bit drab really, with some
Hollywood film star posters on the walls. It shows its community
spirit, however, with special offers for pensioners and
contributions to local charities. The steady weekday trade is
mainly working class with a sprinkling of architects, accountants
and the whole gamut of Leith people, who like the uncomplicated
atmosphere and friendly banter. At the weekends they put on
karaoke nights which are popular. They have disabled toilets in
the lounge which is just being refurbished. Prices are very good
indeed.

Lorrie McGuire's Duke Street *Free House*   K13

M-S 10am-1am, Sun 12.30pm-1am
A refreshing twist on a supposed Irish theme pub. The Irishness
seems to consist of a coat of green paint on the walls and a lot
of Irish rebel songs on the juke box. This big shoebox of a place,
with two raised areas in the corners over the bar (one with a pool
table, the other for dancing) is in fact a Celtic football supporters'
bar – which accounts for the semi-Irishness of the place. With
keg beers, premium lagers and all spirits at very reasonable
prices, they also stock a range of Irish whiskies. Originally part of
the old Leith Railway Station, they put on DJs and karaoke at the
weekends which brings in a large female clientele. The customers
are primarily local residents and this is a clean and bright bar
with a friendly atmosphere. They have disabled toilets.

Central Bar Leith Walk *Tenancy*   K14

M-Th 9am-11pm, FS 9am-1am, Sun 12.30pm-7pm
One of Edinburgh's real treasures, the Central Bar has had a run
of bad luck over the past decade. Closed for a while after a
disastrous fire, it has opened and closed a few times due to a

variety of difficulties. Now under new management, this classic
Victorian bar is hopefully set for a fairer future. They will soon be
installing real beers, though at the moment are restricted to cask
beers and lagers with a limited range of malt whiskies and other
spirits. Prices are fine for the area, helped by a Happy Hour from
5pm-7pm and all day Sunday. They do special prices for OAPs
and currently have no food on offer. The great thing about the
Central is the decor. While possibly not as ostentatious as the
Café Royal, it features a magnificent example of Victorian tiling.
The glorious plasterwork ceiling soars over beautiful cornices and
walls that are entirely covered in tiles. Decorated panels have
floral and radial patterns alternating in beautiful rich pastel
colours. In amongst them are beautifully painted hunting scenes.
Round the entire room there is a frieze of flowers. The windows
retain original leaded, coloured glass, and behind the U-shaped
bar is a remarkable glass-fronted gantry – although very small in
comparison with others, this one has four beautifully carved
griffins carved on it. The bar retains some of the original gas
lamp fittings, converted to electricity. Add in fine wooden seated
booths, some with original cast iron legged tables, and this box
of a room is a visual delight and a truly historical reminder of
Victorian magnificence. Toilets are fine but access is a bit difficult.

Mac's Bar Junction Street *Tenancy*   K15

M-Sat 9am-12am, Sun 12.30pm-11pm
This is a mainly tasteful Art Deco inspired bar near the bottom of
Leith Walk. With keg beers, a dozen or so malt whiskies and a
range of bottled beers and spirits, there is nothing unusual about
the provision of drink. Prices though are very good, and they have
Happy Hours on Wednesday, Thursday and Friday afternoons but
serve no food. Some of the wood fittings, like the bar pillars, are
pleasant, and the room at the back is subtly decorated and
comfortable. The stained glass panels however are best
described as garish. A standard city pub, Mac's has a surprisingly
relaxed atmosphere. The crowd here are mostly workers and
couples during the week, with a younger crowd at weekends,
though even on weekdays there are young folk in attendance.
They tend to focus on television sports from time to time. Toilets
fine and accessible.

Anderson's Henderson Street *Free House*   K16

M-Th 11am-11pm, FS 11am-12am, Sun 12.30pm-10.30pm
Anderson's is a fine wee local back street bar. With a range of
keg beers and pretty standard provision of spirits at very
affordable prices, this is a bar that serves its local community.

They don't do food. A light and clean place with tartan wallpaper,
the bar has a sporting motif throughout, which clearly shows that
golf in Scotland is not restricted to the middle class. There is a
small lounge and a pool room off the bar. The posters and prints
on the walls all reflect the sporting motif, which is underlined by
a glass case full of trophies behind the bar. The customers are
vociferous in their praise for the bar and claim that the beer is of
the very best. Many regulars return after leaving the area and the
place is popular with women and couples too. Toilets fine and
accessible.

The Vintage Henderson Street *Tenancy*   K17

M-S 11am-1am, Sun 12.30pm-1am
Another Leith back street bar near the Shore, this is a fine, big,
local pub which retains some of the history of its 100 years
existence. With a fine old gantry, a long curved bar, some leaded
glass, original cornices, a plasterwork ceiling and a roaring coal
fire, even during the day there is bit of a buzz here. Recently
refurbished, it is sparse, but its still a comfortable place. It is
frequented by a group of fly-fishermen who call themselves the
Reservoir Dogs. For some reason this made the Fifer feel at
home. At the weekends they put on live music of the MOR variety.
It can get a bit crowded but the mainly masculine weekday crowd
improves with a bit of feminine input. The steady local clientele
includes a regular domino playing fraternity and a lot of good
Scottish sarcasm is on show. Toilets alright, but no disabled
access.

The Black Swan Quayside Street *Tenancy*   K18

M-Sat 11am-1am, Sun 12.30pm-2am
This is a very pleasant looking bar occupying the ground floor of a
well-restored Victorian tenement building near the Shore. The
original bar sign is carved into the stonework of the building. The
bar itself has been refurbished at various times and still has an
interesting panelled ceiling with some fantastic carved bosses. It
has a small lounge through the back with a pool table. Beers are
keg and the range of spirits are pretty standard. Prices are
cheap. They have no facilities for food. The customers are mainly
local people, but it gets a bit busier at the weekends. This is a
pub where the management would like to go a bit upmarket. It
could do with money being spent on it – the potential is obvious.
Amenities fine and accessible.

The Ship The Shore *Free House*   K2

> M-W 12pm-11pm, ThF 12pm-1am, S 11am-1am, Sun 11am-11pm
> Overlooking the Water of Leith, this bonny pub seems to be
> changing itself into more of a restaurant – part of the ongoing
> gentrification of the old port, no doubt.

The Waterline The Shore *Managed*   K6

> M-Th 12pm-12am, FS 12pm-1am, Sun 12.30pm-12am
> Always a grand place to eat and with a good line in drink,
> changes are afoot here and awaited with eagerness.

Minto's Duke Street *Free House*   K12

> M-S 11am-11pm, Sun 12.30pm-11pm
> Pretty standard local pub with good prices, darts boards and pool
> table to while away the afternoons. Functional and friendly.

MIXTER-MAXTER

Edinburgh has many fine pubs and not all of them can be grouped together. The following is a selection of one-offs. Most are reachable by the city bus services, and all are within the bounds of the city. Some, like the Sheep's Heid, are absolute historical jewels while others, like the Diggers, have a different sort of history entirely. The Starbank down by the Forth is great on a summer's day, looking over the river. Like the Old Chain Pier just along from it, it is an exciting location to watch storms. This book could probably be twice the current size, but time, money and the poor state of the author's liver necessitated some sort of limit. While the very idea of drinking and driving is absolute anathema, some of these places are worth driving your friends to for lunch. While you sit sipping an orange juice, you can take delight in their increasing silliness as they quaff the ales, whiskies, wines or other beverages of their choice.

Starbank Inn Granton *Managed*   **L1**

M-Th 11am-11pm, FS 11am-12am, Sun 12.30pm-11.30pm
Overlooking the River Forth in Granton, the Starbank Inn is a
testament to what can be done with sympathetic development.
Originally a tiny one roomed bar in a block of cottages, it is now a

spacious and luxurious traditional style bar that has a reputation for quality. They stock ten cask ales in prime condition, and a whisky and wine list of around two dozen each: like a few other places, there are written menus for both whisky and wine. Food is top quality pub grub, all cooked in-house and available from 12pm-2.30pm and 6m to 9pm during the week and all day at the weekends. Around behind the bar is a conservatory full of chairs and tables, used primarily as a dining area. As with the beer, the prices are reasonable, if not cheap. Although the bar and gantry are not original, they are very traditional in style, with a brass foot rail at the bar and an interesting pillared gantry. The tiled fireplace is original, from one of the original colony-style cottages. The decor mixes brewing and nautical motifs with some witty three dimensional wooden wall pieces and a plethora of old beer mats, water jugs and trays – many advertising long gone beverages. This is a place that attracts a lot of business people, a steady core of locals, people who like beer and a growing, if still small number of tourists. Once a month they have Sunday afternoon live jazz. Amenities fine but there are steps into the bar.

Bennet's Bar Maxwell Street *Free House*   L4

M-S 11am-12pm, Closed Sundays
Run by the original owner of Bennet's in Tollcross, this is an entirely different type of pub. Primarily a local bar, they have six cask ales, a selection of 73 different malts and otherwise the standard range of beverages. Food is limited to filled rolls. With a subdued 1930s style decor that has hardly changed over the years, the feeling here is of comfort and continuity. Most of the customers are male, but women are made welcome. Bennet's attracts a mature rather than young crowd, and is clearly a fine community bar. They attract a fair bit of passing trade and a lot of staff from the local hospital. This is a pub that is rarely empty, but never really noisy – though they occasionally have folk acts. A simple, subtle and satisfying hostelry. Amenities are fine but no disabled access.

The Canny Man's Morningside Road *Free House*   L5

M-W 11.30am-12am, Th-S 11.30am-1am, Sun 12.30pm-12am
There is no other pub like the Canny Man's. Established in 1871 as an inn, it has developed in a unique fashion. The exterior of the building hosts various pieces of cast-iron panels, some referring to the old steam railways, while the walls and ceilings of the various rooms inside are covered with a riotous divergence of ephemera, including paintings, carpenters' tools, dentists' tools, clocks, oars and all sorts of stuff amassed over the years. None

of the bits and pieces have been purchased, mainly they have been given as gifts by patrons and friends. Despite, or perhaps because of this glorious clutter, the place has a comfortable atmosphere. Very much an upmarket drinking den, the Canny Man's has hundreds of malt whiskies, dozens of champagnes and vintage wines, and an extensive selection of rums, American bourbons, brandies, vodkas and tequilas, as well as a selection of cask ales. Prices are expensive, and if you are that way inclined you can pay over three hundred smackers for a bottle of red. The menu is extremely large, and centres round Smørrebrød, fancy Scandinavian sandwiches. Food is available daily till 3pm. The management still see themselves as a pub first and foremost, and they specialise in high quality cigars, making a feature of this particular indulgence. They also have a beer garden out back. Although the Canny Man's pays a lot of attention to choice, quality and service, no place that has a sign at the door saying 'Dress Smart But Casual' could ever get top rating – not only do they want your money, but they tell you how to dress before they'll take it. Amenities fine and accessible.

The Golden Rule Yeaman Place *Chain*   L7

M-Th & S 11am-11.30pm, F 11am-12am, Sun 12.30pm-11pm
Beer is the rule here. With four in house and four guest ales, the Rule is known for the quality of its ale. Additionally, they stock 15 malts and a dozen wines, all at very good prices. Food is limited to good quality pies and snacks all day. They make a feature of Belgian Genever (gin) which they serve with a variety of fruit juices at £3.00 a double – yum, yum. Divided into a main saloon bar, with bar stools and bench seating, and a smaller lounge down a short flight of stairs, this is an impeccably kept pub. The decor is modern, traditionally derived saloon bar: dark, sedate and subtle without being pretentious. An obvious magnet for city beer heads, and others from all over this island, the Rule also has a steady local clientele. The lounge attracts women and couples in the week, but at weekends it becomes a bit friskier with a younger crowd and students. While the bar has a no music policy (three cheers), the lounge does have a juke box. They have resorted to having the odd quiz night and there is a television. A slight sporting tendency can be noticed when Heart of Midlothian football team are playing at nearby Tynecastle. Then the place fills up with Jambos, as they are called, though their city rivals the Hibernian fans might add a colourful term or two to the name. This bar is pleasant and welcoming at all times and the beer is very well kept – just the sort of place to go for a pint or two and leave with a spring in your step a few hours later. Amenities are fine and relatively accessible.

The Athletic Arms Ardmillan Terrace *Managed*   L6

M-S 11am-12am, Sun 12.30pm-6pm
Known to generations of city natives as the Diggers', due to its
proximity to a large cemetery and thus the place where
gravediggers slaked their thirst, this fine old pub is to some
extent living on its past reputation. This was the only bar in the
world where, on entering the crowded bar, you could raise two
fingers to the bar staff and not be ejected! In fact, you would
then make your way through the crush to find two pints of
McEwan's Heavy awaiting you on the bar. Such was the fame of
the beer that no words were necessary. Heavy has long been
superseded by 80 shilling ale – its offspring – and a host of other
cask conditioned niceties, but the flavour of Diggers' beer still
evokes nostalgia in those of us who remember it. Rumour has it
that there might be a revival in the offing. The Diggers' nowadays
has four cask ales and stocks a dozen malts, along with the
usual suspects. Snacks and pies are available throughout the
day. Though not a fancy tiled palace, this 1890s bar retains its
originality intact and they have photographs to prove it. The
separating screen between the serving bar and the long bar (a
kind of snug), is leaded glass and ornate wood. The bar has kept
its original small two legged tables, ensuring that drinkers carry
their glasses back to the bar. The curving bar has retained the
original brass water taps. The decor in the bar and back room is
enhanced by portraits of famous Heart of Midlothian football
players down the years. Prices are extremely reasonable and the
clientele of locals and visitors are attracted by the reputation.
Busy on match days. No disabled access to the gents, but the
wheelchair bound can use the ladies.

The Sheep's Heid The Causeway *Managed*   L14

M-W 11am-11pm, Th-S 11am-12am, Sun 12.30pm-11pm
If any pub deserves to be made a national shrine, then this is it.
Set in the historic village of Duddingston, tucked below the
southern slopes of Arthur's Seat, there has been an inn here for
at least half a millennium. The pub was named after a snuff box
made in the shape of a sheep's head, presented to the pub by
James VI before he deserted to London. It was visited by various
royalty and wannabes including Mary Queen of Scots, and that
much romanticised gentleman Bonnie Prince Charlie, who stayed
in the area for a while. Such royal connections in no way diminish
the charms of this braw place. The curved bar, the leaded glass
wooden partitions in between the bench seating, the brass water
taps on the bar, the plain panelled walls, and the comfortable

back room, are all just fine. With china plates and figurines, prints and paintings, the place has all the feel of a first-class but homely country hotel. Pride of place goes to the oil painting of the nearby Battle of Prestonpans in 1745 and the carved sheep's head on the fine gantry. As they have a very reasonable bistro upstairs, the bar food menu is excellent, very affordable and on from 12.30pm-8pm. Prices for the well kept beer are reasonable. Out the back there is a beer garden, behind one wall of which runs their famous skittle alley. With two lanes, this is regularly booked out by parties. It serves as a local pub for a total mix of people; advocates and van drivers, shopkeepers and politicians. It has a steady stream of tourists, mainly from March to November. Although they attract a lot of couples, it is not unusual to find a crowd of young people soaking in the atmosphere on a late Thursday afternoon – and having a whale of a time. Disabled toilets.

Porter's Bar Piershill Terrace *Free House*   L13

M-F 11am-11pm, S 11am-1am, Sun 12.30pm-11pm
Formerly the Piershill Tavern, this was another fine old pub renowned for its beer. Today it retains much of the look and feel of former times and has a couple of real ales and a stock of 80 malts. They regularly have drinks promotions and put on special offers for pensioners. Food is filled rolls. A quietish local bar, it has a wealth of superb leaded glass panels, one still having an original painted bird. The original gantry is stacked with whisky bottles and a coal fire still blazes in the fireplace. The main bar room is half-panelled and the many prints have a sporting motif. Prices are cheap and they attract a mixed crowd including local office workers and a few CAMRA types, but mainly local regulars. Bands play on Saturdays and there is a happy hour 7pm-9pm. Amenities accessible and fine.

Jock's Lodge London Road *Tenancy*   L11

M-W 11am-11pm, Th-S 11am-12am, Sun 12.30pm-5.30pm
This could be the role model for the term cheap and cheerful. Last re-modelled in the 1930s, it has a range of cask beers and lagers and 30 malts at very low prices. It is very popular. Behind the long bar is a big lounge where lunches are served 12pm-2.30pm. Food is standard pub grub, but all home made and incredibly cheap. The prices and atmosphere in the long main bar, decorated with prints and licensed trade odds and ends, bring in office workers from the government agency next door and a fair passing trade, but few tourists. At the moment it's popular with workmen from the Parliament site. It also has good trade from locals and couples, and the staff say this is place you can

hear yourself speak, though the lounge has a juke box. Amenities fine but difficult access.

The Old Chain Pier Trinity Crescent *Tenancy*   L2

M-Th 12pm-11pm, FS 12pm-12am, Sun 12.30pm-11pm
Built on the site of the original bar that was threatening to fall into the river, this new built pub has a good reputation for both food and drink.

Dylan's Party Bar Piershill Place *Free House*   L12

M-W 11am-11pm, T-S 9am-1am, Sun 12.30pm-1am
This place seems to combine sporting activity with go-go-girls and strippers, so it's a fair bet to think of it as a male only type boozer.

Station Bar Cadzow Place *Free House*   L11

M-W 11am-11pm, T-S 11am-12am, Sun 12.30pm-11pm
Very much a local pub that has darts and dominoes teams, this is a friendly and welcoming, unassuming pub.

The Hermitage Comiston Road *Managed*   L3

M-S 11am-11.30pm, Sun 12.30pm-11pm
In Morningside, generally thought of as very posh, this is very much a working class man's bar that has a fine view out over the district.

Bridge Inn Baird Road *Free House*   L15

M-Th 12am-11pm, F 12pm-12am, S 11am-12pm, Sun 12.30pm-11pm
Situated on the Union Canal, this is a country hotel style place with a big reputation for quality. Boats can be hired.

The Roseburn Bar Roseburn Terrace   L8

M-W 9am-11pm, Th-S 9am-12am, Sun 12.30pm-11pm
Near Murrayfield rugby stadium, this is a good example of a traditional Scottish bar with a very high reputation for the quality of its ales.

The Artisan Abbeyhill *Free House*   L9

M-W 11am-11pm, Th-S 11am-11.45pm, Sun 12.30pm-11pm
An interesting building on two floors the Artisan is a fine local pub that can get very busy on match days when the Hibs are at home.

SCOTTISH DRINK

Around the world, Scotland is famous for a few things; tartan, bagpipes, Robert Burns and his sublime poetry and song, but probably above all for its whisky. The French have their brandy, the Russians their vodka, Italians like grappa, Spaniards go blind on various insane absinthes which are somewhat akin to Greek ouzo or Turkish raki, but nothing is quite like whisky – the finest spirit of them all. This is not just bias, for all over the world there are whisky afficionados and societies. However, Scotland has a lot more than whisky to offer. For centuries, due to the Auld Alliance with France, we had a deep love of red wine – a love that burns stronger again these days through our indigenous wines created from such diverse substances as elderflowers, strawberries, birch bark and that most sublime of mountain fruits, the blaeberry. We might occasionally provide super vintages, but we will never match the produce of other, sunnier lands. Within our borders we create a range of beers that is unique and remarkable. Although in these global days much of the licensed trade is dominated by big breweries, with their constant attempts to put small pubs and brewers out of business, there are still a few smaller companies that thrive. And it must be said that even the biggest of the brewers have been forced to produce cask conditioned ales, traditionally brewed and fermented for a second time either in the barrel or bottle, as a result of public demand.

Beer

Scottish beer has traditionally been dark and strong and the most common strength, 80 shilling ale, is about 3.8% ABV. This was the strength of the standard heavy beer which was the staple before keg beer was invented. The name is based on the old price of a barrel of beer and 80 shillings is equivalent to £4.00 nowadays, just about enough for 2 pints in Edinburgh. Additionally there were 60, 70 and 90 shilling ales, the latter being particularly handy for rattling the brain. Today, several brewers make these but there are also a lot of varieties so the standard is not so rigid. The last two decades have seen successful smaller breweries compete with the giants in Scotland. It is worth mentioning Caledonian Ales in Edinburgh, whose Deuchar's IPA or Imperial Pale Ale is becoming an absolute necessity for most real ale bars, and Broughton Ales in the Borders, who have made a good range of draught and bottled beers for many years now, including the lovely and rich Oatmeal Stout. The Orkney Brewery has made a remarkable impact with its delightful – and powerful – Dark Island and the even more mind-blowing Skullsplitter. The

Inveralmond brewery at Perth has been bringing in a range of interesting, often hoppy beers, while Harviestoun impresses with its range. Additionally, apart from longer established creators of very fine ales like Belhaven and Maclays, there are quirky companies like Traquair whose output of bottled strong ale is appreciated across the globe. Fraoch is a newish beer, flavoured with heather derived from a Pictish recipe from more than a millennium ago! The market is dominated by Scottish & Newcastle, and the other big British companies combine to play a large role. While some of them do produce decent beer they can never match the quality of smaller production runs created with care and consideration and lacking the obscene obsession with the bottom line.

Whisky

There are hundreds of Scotch whiskies on the market, all descended from the old Scottish tradition of malting barley, brewing it and then distilling it. In the 18th and 19th Centuries the government battled ferociously to put a stop to the production of 'Peatreek'; during the making of this particular kind of whisky the bothies were filled with smoky peat. By mid 19th Century, in their pursuit of ever greater tax revenues, the government had demolished what for a long time was a thriving cottage industry. Today, whisky is divided into malts and blends. Malts are whiskies distilled from a single type of malted barley, left to mature in sherry or bourbon casks for periods no less than 8 years. Blend whisky is a mix of different malt distillations with those of other grains, and needs to be matured for no more than 3 years. Generally speaking, with both malt and blend whisky, the longer they spend maturing in the cask the better they are – which is why 25 year old malts are so expensive! While blended whisky is palatable, a good single malt is the absolute apogee of distilling. Today there are hundreds of different malts – many created very recently and given spurious historicity by a Gaelic name. However, many of these are superb and now there are even cask-strength whiskies on the market. This is traditionally the whisky coming out of the maturing barrels at 60% ABV, before being diluted to 40% ABV. The difference may be subtle at first, but be careful when drinking cask strength. Again, these days whisky production is in the hands of giant international conglomerates whose only connection to Scotland is through their relentless pursuit of profit. However, it has to be said the quality is high in most cases; bad whisky doesn't sell, though cheap whisky does. Malts are generally divided into three main areas; Highland, Lowland and Island, the variations in the water between different parts of the country being a significant factor. However, a whisky distilled in one glen is in the main quite distinctive from another coming from a glen just a few miles away, such is the skill of its manufacture and variation in the choice of ingredients.

Should you have the misfortune to encounter the author of this little volume in an Edinburgh hostelry, please note that his favourite malts are Dalmore, Glenfarclas, Balvenie, The Glenlivet and The Macallan.

Irn Bru

A Scottish soft drink, 'made from girders', that out-sells Coke in Scotland (Coke and Pepsi are the best sellers in almost every nation on the planet), this is the traditional West Coast remedy for alcoholic over indulgence. Here on the east we may have long resisted its advance, but we can no longer challenge its claim to be Scotland's other national drink, its origins in the Other Place (Glasgow) notwithstanding.

INDEX OF PUB NAMES

Some other books published by LUATH PRESS

FOLKLORE

Scotland: Myth, Legend and Folklore
Stuart McHardy
ISBN: 0 946487 69 3 PBK 7.99

The Supernatural Highlands
Francis Thompson
ISBN 0 946487 31 6 PBK £8.99

Tall Tales from an Island
Peter Macnab
ISBN 0 946487 07 3 PBK £8.99

Tales from the North Coast
Alan Temperley
ISBN 0 946487 18 9 PBK £8.99

ON THE TRAIL OF

On the Trail of William Wallace
David R. Ross
ISBN 0 946487 47 2 PBK £7.99

On the Trail of Robert the Bruce
David R. Ross
ISBN 0 946487 52 9 PBK £7.99

On the Trail of Mary Queen of Scots
J. Keith Cheetham
ISBN 0 946487 50 2 PBK £7.99

On the Trail of Robert Burns
John Cairney
ISBN 0 946487 51 0 PBK £7.99

On the Trail of Robert Service
GW Lockhart
ISBN 0 946487 24 3 PBK £7.99

On the Trail of John Muir
Cherry Good
ISBN 0 946487 62 6 PBK £7.99

NEW SCOTLAND

Scotland - Land and Power the agenda for land reform
Andy Wightman
foreword by Lesley Riddoch
ISBN 0 946487 70 7 PBK £5.00

Old Scotland New Scotland
Jeff Fallow
ISBN 0 946487 40 5 PBK £6.99

Notes from the North incorporating a Brief History of the Scots and the English
Emma Wood
ISBN 0 946487 46 4 PBK £8.99

SOCIAL HISTORY

Shale Voices
Alistair Findlay
foreword by Tam Dalyell MP
ISBN 0 946487 63 4 PBK £10.99
ISBN 0 946487 78 2 HBK £17.99

Crofting Years
Francis Thompson
ISBN 0 946487 06 5 PBK £6.95

A Word for Scotland
Jack Campbell
foreword by Magnus Magnusson
ISBN 0 946487 48 0 PBK £12.99

LUATH GUIDES TO SCOTLAND

Mull and Iona: Highways and Byways
Peter Macnab
ISBN 0 946487 58 8 PBK £4.95

South West Scotland
Tom Atkinson
ISBN 0 946487 04 9 PBK £4.95

The West Highlands: The Lonely Lands
Tom Atkinson
ISBN 0 946487 56 1 PBK £4.95

The Northern Highlands: The Empty Lands
Tom Atkinson
ISBN 0 946487 55 3 PBK £4.95

The North West Highlands: Roads to the Isles
Tom Atkinson
ISBN 0 946487 54 5 PBK £4.95

WALK WITH LUATH

Mountain Days & Bothy Nights
Dave Brown and Ian Mitchell
ISBN 0 946487 15 4 PBK £7.50

The Joy of Hillwalking
Ralph Storer
ISBN 0 946487 28 6 PBK £7.50

Scotland's Mountains before the Mountaineers
Ian Mitchell
ISBN 0 946487 39 1 PBK £9.99

LUATH WALKING GUIDES

Walks in the Cairngorms
Ernest Cross
ISBN 0 946487 09 X PBK £4.95

Short Walks in the Cairngorms
Ernest Cross
ISBN 0 946487 23 5 PBK £4.95

FICTION

The Bannockburn Years
William Scott
ISBN 0 946487 34 0 PBK £7.95

The Great Melnikov
Hugh MacLachlan
ISBN 0 946487 42 1 PBK £7.95

Grave Robbers
Robin Mitchell
ISBN 0 946487 72 3 PBK £7.99

NATURAL SCOTLAND

Wild Scotland: The essential guide to finding the best of natural Scotland
James McCarthy
Photography by Laurie Campbell
ISBN 0 946487 37 5 PBK £7.50

'Nothing but Heather!'
Gerry Cambridge
ISBN 0 946487 49 9 PBK £15.00

Scotland Land and People An Inhabited Solitude
James McCarthy
ISBN 0 946487 57 X PBK £7.99

The Highland Geology Trail
John L Roberts
ISBN 0 946487 36 7 PBK £4.99

Rum: Nature's Island
Magnus Magnusson
ISBN 0 946487 32 4 PBK £7.95

Red Sky at Night
John Barrington
ISBN 0 946487 60 X PBK £8.99

Listen to the Trees
Don MacCaskill
ISBN 0 946487 65 0 PBK £9.99

BIOGRAPHY

Tobermory Teuchter: A first-hand account of life on Mull in the early years of the 20th century
Peter Macnab
ISBN 0 946487 41 3 PBK £7.99

Bare Feet and Tackety Boots
Archie Cameron
ISBN 0 946487 17 0 PBK £7.95

Come Dungeons Dark
John Taylor Caldwell
ISBN 0 946487 19 7 PBK £6.95

MUSIC AND DANCE

Highland Balls and Village Halls
GW Lockhart
ISBN 0 946487 12 X PBK £6.95

Fiddles & Folk: A celebration of the re-emergence of Scotland's musical heritage
GW Lockhart
ISBN 0 946487 38 3 PBK £7.95

SPORT

Over the Top with the Tartan Army (Active Service 1992-97)
Andrew McArthur
ISBN 0 946487 45 6 PBK £7.99

Ski & Snowboard Scotland
Hilary Parke
ISBN 0 946487 35 9 PBK £6.99

POETRY

Poems to be read aloud
Collected and with an introduction by Tom Atkinson
ISBN 0 946487 00 6 PBK £5.00

Blind Harry's Wallace
William Hamilton of Gilbertfield
introduced by Elspeth King
ISBN 0 946487 43 X HBK £15.00
ISBN 0 946487 33 2 PBK £8.99

Luath Press Limited
committed to publishing well written books worth reading

LUATH PRESS takes its name from Robert Burns, whose little collie Luath (*Gael.*, swift or nimble) tripped up Jean Armour at a wedding and gave him the chance to speak to the woman who was to be his wife and the abiding love of his life. Burns called one of *The Twa Dogs* Luath after Cuchullin's hunting dog in *Ossian's Fingal*. Luath Press grew up in the heart of Burns country, and now resides a few steps up the road from Burns' first lodgings in Edinburgh's Royal Mile.
Luath offers you distinctive writing with a hint of unexpected pleasures.

Most UK and US bookshops either carry our books in stock or can order them for you. To order direct from us, please send a £sterling cheque, postal order, international money order or your credit card details (number, address of cardholder and expiry date) to us at the address below. Please add post and packing as follows: UK – £1.00 per delivery address; overseas surface mail – £2.50 per delivery address; overseas airmail – £3.50 for the first book to each delivery address, plus £1.00 for each additional book by airmail to the same address. If your order is a gift, we will happily enclose your card or message at no extra charge.

ILLUSTRATION: IAN KELLAS

Luath Press Limited
543/2 Castlehill
The Royal Mile
Edinburgh EH1 2ND
Scotland
Telephone: 0131 225 4326 (24 hours)
Fax: 0131 225 4324
email: gavin.macdougall@luath.co.uk
Website: www.luath.co.uk